# SEEKING MEANING:
## A PROCESS APPROACH TO LIBRARY AND INFORMATION SERVICES

## Information Management, Policy, and Services
### Charles R. McClure and Peter Hernon, Editors

# SEEKING MEANING:
## A PROCESS APPROACH TO LIBRARY AND INFORMATION SERVICES

**Carol Collier Kuhlthau**
*Rutgers University*

ABLEX PUBLISHING CORPORATION
NORWOOD, NEW JERSEY

Second Printing 1994

Copyright © 1993 by Ablex Corporation

Printed in the United States of America


**Library of Congress Cataloging-in-Publication Data**

Kuhlthau, Carol Collier, 1937–
    Seeking meaning : a process approach to library and information
services / by Carol Collier Kuhlthau.
        p.   cm. — (Information management, policy, and services)
    Includes bibliographical references (p.    ) and indexes.
    ISBN 0-89391-968-3. — ISBN 1-56750-019-6 (pbk.)
    1. Reference services (Libraries)—United States.   2. Searching,
Bibliographical.   3. Information retrieval.   4. Research—United
States—Methodology.   I. Title.   II. Series.
Z711.Z84   1992
025.5'2'0973—dc20                                         92-40770
                                                         CIP


Ablex Publishing Corporation
355 Chestnut Street
Norwood, NJ 07648

Dedicated to
The faculty at the Rutgers University
School of Communication, Information and Library Studies
past and present

# Table of Contents

# List of Figures

# List of Tables

# Preface

This book presents a theoretical framework for a process approach to library and information services, and describes a series of studies of the Information Search Process of users. There is a need for counseling in the process of information seeking. The book develops an expanded counseling role for the library and information professional and recommends practical strategies for designing and implementing interventions into the user's process of learning from information access and use.

Many people influenced my thinking during the research and the development of this work. I would like to take this opportunity to mention some of those who were of immeasurable help to me. Thanks to Janet Emig, David Carr, and Don King for being there at the beginning to guide me through the dissertation study; to Betty Turock, Mary George, and Bob Belvin for their instrumental roles in the verification phase of the research; to Joan Durrance, Evelyn Daniel, and Carol Kroll for ongoing conversation about the future roles of librarians; to Nick Belkin, Tefko Saracevic, and Robert Taylor whose work inspired the underlying constructs; to all of the participants in the studies and particularly to the students in the longitudinal studies and the librarians who collected verification data; to the graduate students who worked on various phases of the research: Bonnie Kunsel, Jackie Boss, Mary Jane McNally, and Louise Miller; to the graduate students who helped prepare the manuscript, especially Amanda Spink, Trudy Downs, and Virginia McDonnell; to Chuck McClure who, with Peter Hernon, so thoughtfully edited various drafts of the manuscript; to John Kuhlthau for constant support; and to all of the faculty at Rutgers University School of Communication, Information and Library Studies for providing a rich collaboration of interdisciplinary ideas.

# Introduction

The objective of library and information services is to increase access to resources and information. Basic access is provided through selection, acquisition, and organization of resources, what Shera (1972) called the operational aspects of librarianship. Increased or enhanced access is provided primarily through two services, reference and instruction. Enhanced access encompasses intellectual as well as physical access. Physical access addresses the location of resources and information. Intellectual access addresses interpretation of information and ideas within resources. This book is about library and information services for intellectual access to information and ideas, and the process of seeking meaning.

Library and information science is in transition and in a theory-building phase. A theory is a conceptualization of a complex combination of facts. As the clinical psychologist George Kelly (1963) explains, "A theory may be considered as a way of binding together a multitude of facts so that one may comprehend them all at once" (p. 18). Theory enables us to rise above the seemingly random confusion of everyday life to see patterns and to understand principles on which to base purposeful, productive action. "A theory provides a basis for an active approach to life" (Kelly 1963, p. 18).

The emerging theory of librarianship, like that of other practice-oriented fields, such as law, medicine, management, and education, is firmly entrenched in library and information practice. In practice-oriented fields, theory directly informs practice and is, therefore, extremely practical. Theory enables the practitioner to base practice on general principles rather than depending solely on hunches and intuition. Experience solidly grounded in an understanding of theory is the basis for making sound diagnoses and designing services that respond to dynamic needs of clients.

The most useful theories are generic to human nature and not situation specific. One way to build theory is to look to other fields and disciplines addressing similar problems and situations for theoretical perspectives that may be applied to a particular situation. There is strong evidence that theories are merging and becoming less discipline-specific, providing a rich climate for creative, broad understanding of human endeavors. For librarianship, established theories in thinking and learning offer insight into users' experience and behavior in information-seeking situations. Borrowed theory is only a beginning, however. Only after rigorous testing and investigation in the particular situations of concern can a statement of theory be accepted. A theoretical statement for a particular endeavor, in this case information seeking, transforms the borrowed theory into a framework to apply to practice.

This book proposes a process theory for library and information services. It describes how the theory emerged from a hunch and some borrowed theory through investigation in a series of studies, to a theoretical statement and a framework for services.

The concept of process began with a hunch. As a high school librarian teaching students to do research papers and helping them to find sources for their projects, I noticed that no matter how well the students were oriented to the library and its resources, there was a common pattern of behavior when they came to the library for the first few days of their research. They were confused and disoriented, often expressing annoyance at the assignment, the library, and themselves. Negative feelings were expressed and frustration was apparent. Why was there hesitation to get started, confusion about the task, lack of confidence in ability, and low motivation and interest?

This question was particularly troubling to me. I was trained in the Deweyan philosophy of education, which emphasized that people learn by becoming actively involved in their own learning and reflecting on their experience, and that healthy learning environments accommodate the whole person, feelings, thoughts, and actions. I had studied learning theory, particularly the constructivists' approach, incorporating schema theory as opposed to the behaviorists' or systems approach to learning.

Kelly's Personal Construct Theory (Kelly, 1963) added the affective dimension commonly left out of psychology theory on thinking and learning (most likely because it is difficult to observe and quantify). What I was observing with my students fell squarely in the affective domain. Kelly's explanation was that learning takes place through a process of construction which is an active, confusing complex process of making sense of new experiences. According to Kelly, new information must be reconstrued to fit into our existing system of constructs. Our view of the world is constantly being constructed by new experiences. This process begins with uncertainty which increases as we encounter inconsistencies and incompatibilities within the new information itself and with our previously established constructs. Construction takes place through a process of formulating tentative hypotheses for testing, assessing, defining, refining, and reconstruing. Ultimately, new constructs are formed; these alter and expand the existing system — in other words, we learn.

Research into the process of writing, conducted in the early 1970s, revealed that people experience phases of composing over time. This work, however, concentrated on writing from what was already known or from long-term memory, and did not address composing from what we learn from information (Emig, 1971; Stotsky, 1990). It occurred to me that there might be a research process with phases similar to those of composing, in which people learn from information. The research process occurs prior to the writing process, essentially in preparation for writing and presenting ideas. This would indicate a formulation phase within the process of information seeking that might be experienced in much the same way that Kelly described the early phase of construction by confusion, doubt, frustration, and even threat. The information-seeking behavior of the students that I was observing supported this notion.

Borrowed theory was a critical element in moving my thinking along to form a hypothesis for empirical testing. The borrowed theory could not be applied directly to the information-seeking behavior, however, without rigorous examination in actual situations of information seeking and use. The borrowed theory provided a frame or lens for viewing the problem at hand. It offered an explanation and perspective for study. But research needed to be conducted to see if the borrowed theory could become grounded theory for information seeking and for application in library and information services.

At that point, I had a concrete image in my mind of people in a particular predicament and some borrowed theory to frame my problem from which to form a hypothesis. The hypothesis was that information seeking is a process of construction that begins with uncertainty and anxiety. The user's experience in the process of information seeking needed to be carefully investigated to test the hypothesis.

Qualitative methods opened the problem for exploration. A study was designed that would uncover the problem for investigation and collect data to be analysed within the frame of constructivist theory, specifically Kelly's personal construct theory.

A group of 25 college-bound high school seniors was studied over a period of one academic year as they worked on two research papers. Some qualitative methods, such as observation, interview, journals, short pieces of writing, timelines, and flow charts, were combined with a method for surveying with a before and after questionnaire eliciting perceptions of information seeking. The result was overlapping data from which common patterns could be identified. The borrowed theory was critical for analyzing the data and establishing patterns. Without this frame, the model that emerged would have lacked a theoretical or generalizable perspective. It would have been difficult, if not impossible, to recognize patterns or gain insight into what was contained in the data without this borrowed theory.

Common patterns that matched Kelly's description of a constructive experience did emerge from the data. Uncertainty, confusion, frustration, and doubt were present early on. As thoughts became clearer, feelings became more confident and controlled. After considerable reflection and thoughtful analysis, six stages were identified in what came to be called the Information Search Process (ISP).

The stages of the Information Search Process were characterized by three realms: the affective (feelings), the cognitive (thoughts), and the physical (actions). The task considered most appropriate to move the process on to the subsequent stage was also identified. The six stages and their predominant tasks were Initiation, to recognize a need for information; Selection, to identify and select the general topic to be investigated; Exploration, to investigate information on the general topic in order to extend personal understanding; Formulation, to form a focused perspective of the topic from the information encountered; Collection, to gather information related to the focused topic; and Presentation, to complete the search and prepare to present or use the findings.

Exploration was the most difficult stage for users, particularly when they attempted to move into the Collection stage immediately after Selection. Collection strategies, such as making a comprehensive search of all sources or taking copious detailed notes, did not work well in this formative stage. Rather, more exploratory strategies, such as listing important facts and interesting ideas or finding a few sources and settling in to read and reflect, were more appropriate for the task at hand. Intentionally seeking a focused perspective within the general topic was essential during this period of information seeking. The focus served as a guiding idea for the search throughout the Collection stage. Interest, which was not particularly high at the beginning of a search, was found to increase considerably after Formulation.

Students were anxious to talk about their process and disturbed that no one had asked them or helped them earlier in their education. The necessity for process intervention to help in the difficult tasks of Exploration and Formulation was apparent. Once the students were in the Collection stage, their searches proceeded more smoothly and more as they expected.

The model was interesting and useful for speculating, but it needed to be verified in several ways before general statements could be made about implications for library and information services. One way to verify findings is to investigate results over time using longitudinal methods. The original group offered an excellent opportunity for longitudinal study. Twenty of the 25 in the original sample responded to a questionnaire inquiring about their perceptions of information seeking after four years of undergraduate study. In addition, 4 of the 6 original case study participants (students interviewed periodically throughout the high school study) were available for follow-up interviews. The longitudinal studies verified the critical components of the model of the Information

Search Process. The students expected a topic to change and a theme to emerge during information seeking. Furthermore, they expected to become more interested as the information seeking progressed. Case study interviews revealed an understanding of the stages in the search process and a tolerance for the ambiguity and uncertainty at the beginning. These students also showed a sense of ownership in the process and the strategies that they used to work through the stages. They showed an awareness of being involved in seeking meaning by purposefully engaging in "focusing and narrowing" and seeking "a thread," "a story," and "an answer to all my questions."

Another way to verify a model built on a small-scale study is through large-scale quantitative methods. Two studies of large, more diverse groups were conducted: one of three levels of high school seniors—high, middle, and low achievers, and another of library users in three types of libraries, academic, public, and school. The findings revealed a similar process across various types of library users. The affective symptoms of uncertainty, confusion, and frustration prevalent in the early stages were associated with vague, unclear thoughts about a topic or problem. As the participants' knowledge shifted to clearer, more focused thoughts, a corresponding shift was noted in feelings of increased confidence and certainty. The model of the Information Search Process was confirmed in these quantitative studies.

A problem surfaced in the large-scale studies, however. When asked to identify the task of each stage, participants chose gathering or completing in every stage over the more exploratory tasks of recognizing, identifying, investigating, and formulating. A "gather and complete" mentality might explain users' expectations after they had selected a topic that they would be able to proceed directly to collection without anticipating a need to explore and formulate. This misunderstanding of tasks within the stages of the search process is likely to result in conflict, particularly in the earlier stages, and may explain the common experience of frustration and anxiety. In the quantitative studies, these stages were referred to in negative terms, such as "procrastinating," rather than more positive explorative terms, such as "mulling," "reflecting," and "learning."

From these studies, a process theory can be derived out of the framework of the borrowed theory. An articulation of a process theory of information seeking was developed and proposed as the uncertainty principle. The theoretical statement is based on the constructivist view of learning as it was revealed in the studies of the Information Search Process. An uncertainty principle is proposed for information seeking on which to base library and information services. The uncertainty principle is defined thusly:

> Uncertainty due to a lack of understanding, a gap in meaning, a limited construct initiates the process of information seeking. Uncertainty is a cognitive state that commonly causes affective symptoms of anxiety and lack of confidence. Uncertainty and anxiety can be expected in the early stages of the Information Search Process. The affective symptoms of uncertainty, confusion, and frustration are associated with vague, unclear thoughts about a topic or question. As knowledge states shift to more clearly focused thoughts, a parallel shift is noted in feelings of increased confidence.

Six corollaries further define the basic postulate: Process Corollary, Formulation Corollary, Redundancy Corollary, Mood Corollary, Prediction Corollary, and Interest Corollary.

The process theory for library and information services, as stated in the uncertainty principle, indicates a need for redefining the two traditional services of reference and user education. In order to redefine services for intellectual access to resources and information, intervention with users may be conceptualized as occurring on different levels.

In this book, both reference and instruction services have been differentiated into five levels of intervention. These levels describe the intervention of the information professional into the user's information-seeking process in order to enhance intellectual access. The role of librarians in reference service is redefined as five levels of mediation: Organizer, Locator, Identifier, Advisor, and Counselor. In a similar way, the role of those involved in instruction is redefined as five levels of education: Organizer, Lecturer, Instructor, Tutor, and Counselor. At the lowest level (Organizer) and at the highest level (Counselor), the two services, reference/mediation and instruction/education, merge into one.

Once services have been defined within levels of intervention the next step is to identify ways to diagnose users' problems to determine the level of intervention most appropriate for effective service. The concept of a zone of intervention is introduced as an area in which intervention will enable the user to solve his or her information need at a particular point in time. The concept of a zone is borrowed from Vygotsky's (1978) theory related to learning, which states that teaching should be designed for that zone where the child can do with the help of an adult what he or she cannot do alone. Assistance in this zone enables the child to move ahead and get on with his or her own learning. In a similar way, in library and information services the zone of intervention is that zone where the user can do with the help of a librarian what he or she cannot do alone. The assistance enables him or her to move ahead with the task.

Diagnostic intervention is quite common in professions that serve people in problem situations. Other professionals, such as lawyers, physicians, and social workers, diagnose their clients' problems to determine the level of practice required. A model of the physician's approach to diagnosing a patient for treatment is used as a comparison for diagnosing intervention into users' problems in library and information services.

Five zones of intervention into users' problems are identified. In zone one (Z1), the problem is self diagnosed and a search is conducted by the user independent of any intervention by the librarian. In zones two (Z2) through five (Z5), the user's problem is diagnosed through an interview that consists of a problem statement or request and some background information about the task, personal interest, time allotted, and information available. The librarian makes a diagnosis on the basis of theory and experience. The process approach is proposed as a theory to be incorporated into the information professional's frame of reference for making diagnostic judgments of what intervention is required. In zones two (Z2) through four (Z4), the user's problem is diagnosed as requiring product or source intervention. In zone two (Z2) it is determined that one right source is required to solve the user's problem, in zone three (Z3) a group of relevant sources, and in zone four (Z4) a sequence of relevant sources. In zone five (Z5), however, the information professional diagnoses the user's problem as requiring process intervention, which includes entering into an ongoing dialogue and guiding in exploration, formulation, construction, learning, and application in the Information Search Process.

The five zones of intervention into users' problems correspond with the five levels of mediation and instruction. The fifth zone (Z5), calling for process intervention at the Counselor level, is the area which needs further development by library and information professionals. The fifth level of intervention is based on the theoretical perspective incorporating the uncertainty principle.

Schön (1982) describes the experienced professional as a reflective practitioner, who combines theory and professional expertise to create practice. In this way, reflective practitioners need to redefine and revitalize library and information services for the information age. This book is written as a tool for reflective librarians and information professionals to articulate a theoretical perspective for designing intervention services that recognize and respond to users' needs for counseling in the process of learning from information access and use.

The book is divided into 10 chapters. Chapter 1 describes a shift in library and information science from a bibliographic paradigm to users' problems and process revealing the need for building a process theory for library and information science. Chapter 2 discusses the constructivist theory of learning and suggests that information seeking may be studied within this view. The writings of John Dewey provide a historical and philosophical perspective. George Kelly's theory of personal constructs offers a psychological perspective, and Jerome Bruner's research and writings verify the psychological premise and expand the contemporary perspective.

Chapter 3 describes an extensive qualitative study of library users revealing information seeking as a process of construction and presents a six-stage model of the Information Search Process. Chapter 4 describes verification of the model of the information search process in two large scale quantitative studies. Chapter 5 discusses further verification and expansion of the model in two longitudinal studies. Chapter 6 discusses a methodology for studying the user's perspective of information seeking and for building grounded theory of a process approach to information seeking.

Chapter 7 introduces an uncertainty principle, which is a theoretical statement proposing a process theory for library and information services. Chapter 8 discusses implications for library and information services and redefines reference service and user education in five levels of intervention. Chapter 9 presents ways of diagnosing users' problems to determine the level of intervention needed, and the chapter introduces the notion of a zone of intervention as a means for determining level of mediation or education. Chapter 10 summarizes the process approach and suggests ways of intervening in the users' process of learning from information access and use and in their quest for seeking meaning.

# Chapter 1

## The Constructive Process in Library and Information Theory

Traditionally, library and information services have centered on sources and technology. Libraries have developed sophisticated systems for collecting, organizing, and retrieving sources and have applied advanced technology to provide extensive access to vast sources of information. This bibliographic paradigm of collecting and classifying texts and devising search strategies for their retrieval has promoted a view of information use from the system's perspective. Information retrieval has concentrated on what matches the system's representation of texts rather than responding to users' problems and process of information gathering.

While there is no question that the difficulties of controlling increasing quantities of information must continue to be creatively addressed, the individual's process of using information is an integral aspect that cannot be overlooked. Expertly organized library collections may remain untouched without proper linkage to users' problems and process. As Wilson (1977) points out,

> It is not the difficulty of access but the time, effort, and difficulty of using documents that are the major deterrents to library use. (p. 123)

The difficulty of using information is of increasing concern in information provision.

## THEORETICAL FOUNDATIONS OF LIBRARY AND INFORMATION SERVICES

Although the bibliographic paradigm has been the traditional basis of the information profession, the major writings on the theoretical foundations of library and information services have recognized the user's perspective as a critical component in information provision. Shera's (1972) classic text, *The Foundations of Education for Librarianship,* begins with a chapter entitled, "Communication and the Individual," which includes an extensive discussion of learning. In *Library Services in Theory and Context,* Buckland (1983) introduces the notion of the process of "becoming informed" and discusses barriers to the process. Along with indicative and physical access which libraries traditionally emphasize, he includes linguistic and conceptual access which are commonly considered outside the purview of the library or information system. Vickery and Vickery (1981), in *Information Science in Theory and Practice,* address the information needs of everyone by discussing such problems as selective attention and transfer of meaning and by devoting an entire chapter to "People and Information."

In *Public Knowledge, Private Ignorance,* Wilson (1977) directly confronts the issue by juxtaposing the provision for access to what he calls "public knowledge" with the individual's need to learn from information referred to as "personal ignorance." Public knowledge is the view of the world that is the best we can collectively construct at a given time. Personal ignorance, which is our individual need for information, prompts us to tap into the source of public knowledge in one way or another. As he states,

> We each have a set of habits or routines for keeping our internal models of the world up to date and thereby using public knowledge to a greater or lesser extent. (p. 36)

Wilson proposes that libraries and information systems be tailored to the way people use information in their daily lives. "Any policy for library system development should be based on an understanding of individual information gathering behavior" (p. 1). Connections need to be made between the way people use information and the way libraries and information systems provide information.

## TOWARD A GROUNDED THEORY OF THE
## USER'S PERSPECTIVE

Although the authors of these theoretical texts have acknowledged the necessity for considering use of information, each has also noted that little empirical research has been done in this area to provide a basis for a grounded theory of users' information processes. Dervin and Nilan (1986) found that most studies remain constrained by the system's definition of needs, with the menu of responses coming from the system's world and not that of the users. Dervin and Nilan call for researchers to address the user's perspective of information use in order to provide a solid research base on which to build a conceptual framework for both practice and research.

On the whole, user studies, which make up the largest single body of research in librarianship, have been constrained by a narrow view of information use (Dervin and Nilan, 1986). Information is viewed as a thing or product to be given out, the right answer and the right source, rather than for learning and changing constructs. Too often assessments have been confined to a single incident or an answer to a specific question measured in terms of accuracy. Evaluations of outcome based on measures of accuracy of recall are being recognized as inadequate for assessing the complex learning process in which individuals often engage as they search for information. Such judgments may be effective for evaluating a response to a single question but when a person is involved in the dynamic process of becoming informed, relevance does not remain static. What is relevant at the beginning of a search may later turn out to be irrelevant, and vice versa. Therefore, the concept of relevance as a static entity is severely limited for understanding the dynamic process of formulating a problem or learning about a subject.

In extensive breakthrough research, Dervin, Jacobsen, and Nilan (1983) found that when information seeking is viewed as a process of sense making in which a person is forming a personal point of view, an alternative to the narrow single incident is revealed for study. The individual is actively involved in finding meaning that fits in with what he or she already knows, which is not necessarily the same answer for all, but sense making within a personal frame of reference. The person seeks meaning, rather than a right answer, and views information as a way of learning and finding meaning or as a process of construction.

In the active personal process of formulating and learning, an individual's judgments of relevance are difficult to predict and frequently do not match the system's determination of relevance (Saracevic, 1975). Relevance may vary not only from person to person but also from time to time for the same person. Saracevic, Mokros, and Su (1990) suggest that the concept of usefulness is more appropriate for assessing services within the natural process of information seeking. There is a need for methods that take into account changes in relevance, meaning, and understanding, within the process of information seeking.

Research related to human interaction in information systems reveals a shift in emphasis from concentration on the bibliographic paradigm of document or text representations and associated search techniques to the study of users in information-seeking situations (Belkin and Vickery, 1985; Borgman, 1984). The new approach centers on the user's problem in the process of sense making, stressing that effectiveness of information retrieval must consider the integration of results with the user's own life as well as the user's evaluation of the usefulness of the information for the resolution of the problem (James, 1983; Hall, 1981; Ingwersen, 1982). The personal meaning that the user seeks from the information becomes as critical a consideration for library and information services as the content represented in texts (Hollnagel and Woods, 1983; Dervin, 1982; Belkin, 1984; Bates, 1986).

Turning our attention to the user's perspective of information seeking, we become aware of an active personal process. The process of construction within information seeking involves fitting information in with what one already knows and extending this knowledge to create new perspectives. Wilson (1977) defines this type of information use as being motivated by a concern involving a commitment to action which gives structure to information seeking. "A commitment to action automatically provides a basis for classification of information into more, less, or not at all relevant" (p. 44). It is the individual formulation of a personal perspective or focus from the information gathered in order to create something new, at least for him or herself, that fits with the notion of construction.

The constructive process of learning in the library requires services which enable individuals to relate new information to what they already know and extend that knowing to form new understandings. According to Wilson (1977),

> What sets a good library off from other sources of documentary material is its provision not merely of simple summaries for shallow interests but of a complex array of sources from which the individual can piece together for himself what may never yet have been explicitly summarized. (p. 98)

Library services based exclusively on a source/location premise are constrained in situations which call for mediation into the constructive process of users.

## COGNITIVE PROCESS IN INFORMATION SEEKING

The literature of library and information science offers convincing evidence that information seeking is an intellectual process. Recent research reveals information needs as evolving from a vague awareness of something missing and as culminating in the location of information that contributes to understanding and meaning.

Central to the cognitive point of view is what DeMey (1977) refers to as the information processor's model of the world that is determined by prior experience and education. The information science community refers to the constructs held by individuals as knowledge structures which have been described as cognitive maps that shift according to conceptual development (Ingwersen, 1982; Hall, 1981; Meadow, 1983). Stages in the process have been described as occurring in three phases: information seeking, information gathering, and information giving (Krikelas, 1983).

Concentrating on cognitive aspects, Belkin, Brooks, and Oddy (1982) describe the constructive process of information seeking in terms of the ASK (anomalous state of knowledge) hypothesis. An information search begins with the user's problem. The gap between the user's knowledge about the problem or topic and what the user needs to know to solve the problem is the information need. The user's state of knowledge is dynamic rather than static, changing as he or she proceeds in the process. They describe a scale of levels in the ability to specify an information need as beginning with a new problem, in a new situation, in which connections can be made with existing knowledge, and as ending with a defined problem in a well understood situation with an identifiable gap in knowledge. The user's ability to articulate requests to the information system can be expected to change according to his or her level of understanding of the problem. At the lower levels of the specificity scale, questions are most appropriate and experiential needs most apparent. At the upper levels of the specificity scale, requests can be made as commands of *informative* needs (Belkin, 1980). In the initial stages of a problem, specifying precisely what information is needed may be nearly impossible for the user.

Taylor's early work on levels of information need and his more recent writings on value-added information and information use environments, place the user's cognitive process in the forefront of considerations of information provision (Taylor, 1962, 1968, 1986, 1991). He describes four levels of information need evident in users' queries as: *Visceral,* an actual but unexpressed need for information; *Conscious,* a within-brain description of the need; *Formalized,* a formal statement of need; and *Compromised,* the question as presented to the information system.

Taylor also finds that, in the initial stages of a search, users are most likely to express their need for information in the form of questions which make connections with their existing knowledge. Only in the latter stages, after specific gaps in knowledge have been identified, can user requests be expected to be expressed in the form of commands for specific information. However, users seem to employ a less straightforward strategy in actual information-seeking situations. While a continuum may be seen as proceeding from questions, to problems, and to sense making, there do not seem to be definite boundaries between these activities (MacMullin and Taylor, 1984). An intricately interwoven process comprised of mental, physical, and perceptual activities moves the user toward the goal state of sense making.

## AFFECTIVE EXPERIENCE IN INFORMATION SEEKING

The classic triad of thoughts, actions, and feelings so central to any constructive process has not been taken seriously in study or discussion of information-seeking behavior. The user's action taken to gather information has, of course, been established as critical for solving information needs. The cognitive process continues to be increasingly accepted as a significant component for understanding information use. The affective experience, however, has been largely neglected in the literature with a few notable exceptions.

MacMullin and Taylor (1984) conclude that a model representing the user's sense-making process in information seeking ought to incorporate three realms of activity: *physical,* actual actions taken; *affective,* feelings experienced; and *cognitive,* thoughts concerning both process and content. A person moves from the initial state of information need to the goal state of resolution by a series of choices made through a complex interplay within these three realms. The criteria for making these choices are influenced as much by environmental constraints, such as prior experience, knowledge, interest, information available, requirements of the problem, and time allotted for resolution, as they are by the relevancy of the content of the information retrieved. According to Bates (1986), the search process, particularly during the entry and orientation phases, is more subtle and more complex on several grounds than current models assume.

A holistic view of the information user encompassing affective experience as well as cognitive aspects is needed. Wilson (1981) states that interaction between the user and the information system may be guided by both affective needs and cognitive needs. While purely cognitive conceptions of information need are adequate for some research purposes, consideration of the affective dimension of users' problems is necessary for a model to address a wider, holistic view of information use.

## ANXIETY AND UNCERTAINTY IN INFORMATION SEEKING

A number of studies have shown that anxiety accompanies information seeking. Library anxiety (Mellon, 1986), revealed in studies of academic library users, and technology anxiety, revealed in studies of computer users (Borgman, 1984), suggest an association between common feelings of discomfort and information use, particularly in novice users. Both lines of research, however, attribute feelings of anxiety to a lack of familiarity with sources and technology. More may be going on here. Anxiety may be an integral part of the information-seeking process resulting from uncertainty and confusion. Uncertainty is a necessary critical element in any process of construction. When the information search process is viewed as a process of construction, uncertainty and anxiety are anticipated and expected as part of the process.

Another basic characteristic of the process of construction, which offers insight into the anxiety and uncertainty in information seeking, is that we each enter the process with a system of personal constructs built on past experience. Learning in libraries involves a vigorous process of using information in which the learner is actively engaged in seeking meaning from the information he or she gathers as a search progresses. The topic or problem changes and emerges in a series of stages or levels of understanding which are dependent upon not only the information he or she encounters but also the individual's perspective, background, and knowledge. Therefore, the user uniquely creates each search within the framework of his or her personal constructs related to the problem at hand and to his or her larger world view. The concept of an ideal search in an objective sense does not fit into this dynamic, personal, constructive view of information use. Rather, each search is fundamentally different and subjective. The user's personal perspective determines what he or she selects to learn along the way; that perspective directs the search through personal choices of relevance.

## UNCERTAINTY PRINCIPLE

The bibliographic paradigm is based on certainty and order, whereas the users constructive process is characterized by uncertainty and confusion. Several researchers (Whittemore and Yovits, 1973; Bates, 1986) have proposed an uncertainty principle for library and information science. Yet, this concept of an uncertainty principle as a theoretical statement needs further development to include the users' perspective of information seeking.

A more holistic view of information seeking incorporates the experience of interacting thoughts, actions, and feelings in the process of construction. Uncertainty initiates the process, and anxiety and an unsettling discomfort may be expected in the early stages. The principle of uncertainty may include the uncertainty of choices of each individual user within a search for information. It can be concluded then that an information search is a learning process in which the choices along the way are dependent on personal constructs rather than on one universal predictable search for everyone.

Chapter 7 proposes an uncertainty principle as a theoretical foundation for library and information services. While building on the concept of an uncertainty principle, as previously proposed by Whittemore and Yovits (1973), this proposal concentrates on the constructivist theory of learning (see Chapter 2) and the findings of library user studies (see Chapters 3 through 6).

## THEORY TO PRACTICE

Two well-established library services for mediating with information users are reference service and instruction. In recent years, each of these services has shown evidence of: (1) change to accommodate more than simply locating information, and (2) exploring ways to mediate in the use of information, although the bibliographic paradigm remains the primary orientation of library and information services. Further theoretical underpinnings for constructive mediation are sorely needed.

### Reference Services

Katz, long considered the authority on reference services, authors the text used to educate many new librarians for professional practice. An analysis of the presentation of the reference interview in his 1987 edition reveals that he places considerable emphasis on the communication aspects of the interview. This suggests that the core of the interaction centers on open and closed questions. "The open query is general and one which begins with a broad topic. . . . The closed question is restrictive and normally implies an equally specific reply" (p. 49). He considers open and closed questions in terms of the user asking the question and of the librarian responding to the user. Katz recommends that in the reference interview the librarian turn a tight closed question into a relaxed conversation about the topic.

Katz describes three levels of reference service: Conservative or Minimum Service, which may consist of pointing out where a source may be found; Moderate or Middling Service, in which the librarian makes an effort to instruct select patrons in the use of the library while answering their question; and Liberal or Maximum Service, in which the librarian consistently comes up with the answer or with the sources of the answers. The librarian only offers liberal or Maximum Service when such help is requested (pp. 53–54). The dual effect of technology may be expanding direct access to databases and driving the library into the adoption of maximum service as an information mediator.

The reference services described by Katz are firmly established in a source orientation and in the bibliographic paradigm. As Durrance (1989) notes, library and information services have a long way to go toward being fully responsive to the information needs of regular library users without any consideration for the vast unserved. Furthermore,

> Reference services in libraries have, for a century, served primarily to explain a bibliographic apparatus, help users find library materials, and increase access to the information within the library. Has the time come to re-invent reference service so that it is more responsive to user needs? Researchers have begun to question the design of traditional reference service and the messages it sends to library users. The present model, developed when libraries were far more concerned with materials than with people, suffers from a lack of user orientation. (p. 166)

Comparisons of interview techniques of other professionals, such as physicians, have revealed basic differences in the environment in which the interaction takes place. Lynch (1977) points out that the reference interview is conducted in public, that there is rarely any privacy, and that time considerations often force the librarian to cut the interview short: "The context of the reference interview makes it resemble the interview of a sales clerk rather than the interview of the physician or attorney or personnel officer" (pp. 136–137). However, technology also may be changing the environment of the reference interview with the increase of presearch conferences which are scheduled in advance, require a substantial block of time, and are conducted in relative privacy.

## Instruction

Bibliographic instruction in academic libraries has evolved through three models or approaches described by Tuckett and Stoffle (1984): a library tool approach, a conceptual frameworks approach, and a theory-based approach. Library skills instruction in school library media centers has evolved through three similar models or approaches: a source approach, a pathfinder approach, and a process approach (Kuhlthau, 1987). The tool or source approach centers on aiding students to use their particular library and its specific sources by improving their location skills. The conceptual frameworks or pathfinder approach, based on the pioneering work of Patricia Knapp, centers on teaching a search strategy concentrating on both locating and using sources. The Knapp (1966) program was designed to teach students about the library as a system of ways; "whoever would use the system must know the 'way' to use the system. Knowing the way means understanding the nature of the total system, knowing where to plug into it, knowing how to make it work" (Knapp, p. 80). The pathfinder approach is designed to lead students through a sequence of sources in a search to help them to understand the relationship among the sources in the library. Unfortunately, the tool/source approach and the conceptual/pathfinder approach have limited potential for transference to other situations of information seeking. This is due largely to the fact that while source use and location skills are emphasized, the reasoning process that underlies independent learning is not developed. Both approaches "do not typically deal with evaluation of sources or the analysis of information need and do little to create flexible problem solving abilities" (Tuckett and Stoffle, 1984, p. 60).

A new model for instruction concerned with problem solving and learning is emerging. The theory-based process approach involves using, interpreting, and finding meaning in information. Knapp (1966) found that students "have a basic misconception of the function of information inquiry, that they look for and expect to find 'the answer to the question' instead of evidence to be examined" (p. 283). The underlying theoretical concept proposed by the Knapp project centers on "the intellectual processes involved in retrieval of information and ideas" (Lindgren, 1982, p. 28). The concept of teaching library resources as evidence to be examined for shaping a topic rather than finding a quick answer to a question is the key idea behind problem solving and learning how to learn in the library. "We must concentrate on uniting the processes of gathering information with the uses of information" (p. 31).

The movement toward problem solving in academic libraries parallels the recent emphasis on critical thinking in school libraries. A concept paper by Mancall, Aaron, and Walker (1986) provides the rational for incorporating the development of thinking skills into library instruction. They emphasize that:

> Information management skills instruction . . . must be broad and more process oriented. Focus must go beyond location skills and 'correct answers' and move to strategies that will help students to develop insight and facility in structuring successful approaches to solving information needs. (p. 22)

George's (1990) thorough review of the literature of bibliographic instruction for the last 30 years discloses a serious lack of theoretical underpinnings and some strides in acknowledging the necessity for moving in a more theoretical direction. Several recent papers have delved into the work of Bruner (1973, 1975, 1977, and 1986) for a theoretical foundation applicable to practice. George also notes that only two truly new theories pertaining to instruction have come from research rather than from pure reasoning. One is Mellon's (1986) recognition of library anxiety, derived from qualitative studies using students research logs and interviews. The other is the work reported in the next chapter on the information search process. George (1990) cautions that research that focuses on cognitive development, long-term learning retention, and creativity needs to supplement traditional data-gathering techniques that take snapshots but not movies.

Instruction may need to move away from the goal of developing self-reliant users to one of developing life-long learners. Life-long learners are people who can recognize their information need, understand their constructive process, and know how to work with the system and its mediators. Self-reliance in information systems may not be as important as understanding how and when to work with mediators for information seeking and use. The two primary library services, reference and instruction, actually may be two aspects of the service of intervention for information provision. Mediation and education may be tailored to serve users with a variety of information needs at different levels of intervention.

When information searching is placed in the context of learning, the complex constructive process of using information becomes apparent. Critical questions, related to library services for providing helpful intervention, include: "What do people actually experience in a search for information?" "What are their expectations, purposes, motives, and constructs?" and "What thoughts and feelings prompt their actions as they progress, and how do these interact to form the whole experience of information seeking?"

Before we can address these questions in an empirical way, a more extensive theoretical framework is needed on which to base the analysis of data collected on the user's perspective in information-seeking situations. At present, the theory base in library and information science is not sufficient to explain fully the user's experience. In this theory-building phase, a borrowed theory from a similar area of human endeavor provides a way of expanding the theory base for analysis. A borrowed theory frequently sparks a revelation of a new way of viewing a problem and initiates fresh insights. The next chapter presents the theory of learning as a process of construction and recommends ways of applying the borrowed theory for investigating users in the process of learning from information in libraries.

# Chapter 2

## Learning as a Process

Information seeking is a primary activity of life. People seek information to deepen and broaden their understanding of the world around them. When information seeking in libraries is placed in a larger context of learning, the user's perspective becomes an essential component in information provision. Serious problems arise when the user's experience in the process of learning from information does not match the way the system is designed to provide information. We need to understand the user's perspective in order to design more effective library and information services.

A sound theoretical foundation is necessary for developing effective practice. A theory is a conceptualization of a complex combination of concepts. It offers an articulation of underlying complexity which can be understood, discussed, and acted upon. In practice-oriented fields, theory provides the basis for responsible action. Theory enables us to rise above the seemingly random confusion of everyday life to see patterns and to understand principles on which to base purposeful, productive action.

In order to understand the user's perspective of information seeking it is helpful to delve into the theory of other allied fields, particularly the psychology of learning. This chapter presents a theory borrowed from psychology which explains peoples' experience in the process of learning. We begin with this borrowed theory because we find a lack of theory within library and information science to explain fully the user's perspective of information seeking. The related borrowed theory offers insight into similar human endeavors and provides the basis for developing a grounded theory specifically for information seeking. The borrowed theory offers a frame or lens for viewing the information-seeking behavior of library users.

The constructivist view of learning, which offers insight into what the user experiences, is a particularly valuable way to understand information seeking from the user's perspective. Two basic themes run through the theory of construction. One is that we construct our own unique personal worlds, and the other is that construction involves the total person incorporating thinking, feeling, and acting in a dynamic process of learning. This chapter will consider these themes from both a philosophical and a psychological position within a historical and a contemporary context. The chapter presents a selected view of constructivist theory which provides the theoretical frame of reference for a series of studies of the user's experience in the information-seeking process and for the model which emerged from the findings.

Three prominent theorists on construction are John Dewey, George Kelly, and Jerome Bruner. The particular aspects of their work that relate most directly to information seeking are presented rather than a complete summary of their writings. Each theorist offers a somewhat different perspective of the issue and, thus, fills in the picture from several vantage points. John Dewey provides the philosophical foundation for viewing learning as a constructive process. From the historical perspective, his writings form the foundation for later, more empirical work in psychology. George Kelly, a clinical psychologist, verified and refined the theory of construction from the psychological perspective. His publications in the 1950s and 1960s provided an alternative explanation to the behaviorist description of learning which was pervasive at the time. He expanded the theory by defining a series of feelings associated with the phases of construing and reconstruing. Psychologist Jerome Bruner further verified constructive theory in his research on perception. His recent writings offer a contemporary perspective on learning as a constructive process. This chapter will discuss the compatible concepts within their work and the relation of those concepts to the process of learning from information.

## JOHN DEWEY: A PHILOSOPHICAL AND
## HISTORICAL PERSPECTIVE

In the early decades of the 20th century, John Dewey developed a philosophy of education that was uniquely American. Dewey's constructivist theory of learning was established from a philosophical perspective based on the earlier writings of John Locke. Although Dewey was principally a philosopher not an educator, he recognized the critical role that education plays in a democracy and turned his attention to developing the philosophical foundation of education in a free society. His work has had extensive and lasting impact on educational theory and practice, although some applications of his theories, in the form of progressive education, have not been totally successful. Rereading Dewey's writings today, one finds the ideas refreshingly enlightening and surprisingly relevant.

Dewey (1944) recognized that the basic nature of a democratic society is change and that the principle function of education is to prepare people for change;

> A society which is mobile . . . with change occurring anywhere must see that its members are educated for personal initiative and adaptability. Otherwise they will be overwhelmed by the changes in which they are caught and whose significance of connections they do not perceive. (p. 88)

We have certainly witnessed that the change from an industrial economy to an information society affects those who do not have the knowledge or skills to adapt and who are overwhelmed by the changes in which they are caught. Zuboff's (1988) studies of the automated workplace have revealed a radical change in the skills that all types of workers need. The information age is characterized by the availability of vast amounts of information and rapid changes of events. This dynamic environment calls for people needing abilities beyond basic skills in reading, writing, and computing. They need the higher-level skills of thinking and problem solving.

This leads us to the question: "What is it to be literate in an information society?" While there is no formal consensus on this matter many would respond that knowing how to learn is at the heart of education. Learning how to learn may be understood as individually internalizing a constructivist approach to learning.

## Acting and Reflecting

Dewey (1944) described learning as an active individual process, not something done to someone but rather something that a person does. "Education," he said, "is not an affair of telling and being told but an active and constructive process" (p. 41). The axiom "learning by doing" is often attributed to Dewey. However, that is only half of the equation. The other critical half is thinking or reflecting. Learning takes place through a combination of acting and reflecting on the consequences which Dewey called reflective experience or reflective thinking. Through reflection we seek connections between our actions and the results. In this way, we achieve a deep understanding that is transferable to a range of situations. Transference is the ultimate objective of education. Education is "the power to retain in one's experience something which is of value in coping with the difficulties in a later situation" (Dewey, 1944, p. 44). Dewey described learning as a continuous process of reflective experience in which the person is actively constructing his or her view of the world.

Consideration for the whole child was another of Dewey's postulates. Learning takes place within the context of a whole experience in which the learner is completely engaged. A whole experience goes beyond the narrow, one-dimensional, passive incident to encompass actively all aspects of the new. Although Dewey (1934) did not explicitly define the interplay of thoughts, feelings, and actions, his concept of the whole child projects this view. His description of reflective thinking inseparably interweaves three aspects: thoughts, actions, and feelings.

## Phases of Reflective Thinking

In his book, *How We Think,* Dewey (1933) explained the interrelatedness of actions and thoughts. He described what he called reflective thinking as occurring in five phases: Suggestion, Intellectualization, Guiding Idea (Hypothesis), Reasoning, and Testing by Action (pp. 106–114).

The first phase, Suggestion, is a state of doubt due to an incomplete situation characterized by perplexity, confusion, uncertainty, and hesitation. The difficulty is spread throughout the situation and infects the situation as a whole. Direct activity is temporarily arrested. The conditions of hesitation and delay are essential to the job of reflecting on the difficulty.

The second phase, Intellectualization, involves conceptualizing the problem, interpreting the given elements, and anticipating possible solutions and suggestions. The third phase, the Guiding Idea or Hypothesis, is a tentative interpretation of the suggestion that is used as a hypothesis to initiate or guide the collection of factual material. A careful survey incorporating examination, inspection, exploration, and analysis is made to define and clarify the problem at hand. Acts of searching for, hunting for, and inquiring about information characterize this phase.

In the fourth phase, Reasoning, the hypothesis is made more precise and more consistent by familiarity with a wider range of facts. An elaboration of the idea emerges through reasoning. The fifth phase, Testing by Action, involves taking a stand on the projected hypothesis, doing something to bring about results (and thereby testing the hypothesis by overt or imaginative action), and concluding with a resolution of doubt. The result is settling and disposing of the perplexity.

In the five phases of reflective experience (see Table 2–1), Dewey (1933) describes the dynamic role that the individual plays in the process of using information for learning. Extensive thinking and reflection are an integral part of the information-seeking process, for as he wrote:

If we knew just what the difficulty was and where it lay the job of reflection would be much easier than it is. . . . As the saying goes, a question well put is half answered. In fact, we know what the problem

Table 2–1.   Dewey – Phases of Reflective Thinking

| PHASES | DEFINITION |
| --- | --- |
| Suggestion | Doubt due to incomplete situation |
| Intellectualization | Conceptualizing the problem |
| Guiding Idea (hypothesis) | Tentative Interpretation |
| Reasoning | Interpretation with more precise facts |
| Action | Idea tested by overt or imaginative action |

exactly is simultaneously with finding a way out and getting it resolved. Problem and solution stand out completely at the same time. Up to that point, our grasp of the problem has been more or less vague and tentative. (p. 108)

Dewey explains that facts, data, and information arouse ideas that enable the learner to make inferences. In these "leaps from the known" the learner is "going beyond the information given" (p. 158), a phrase later adopted by Bruner.

## GEORGE KELLY: A PSYCHOLOGICAL PERSPECTIVE

While Dewey's writing was primarily philosophical, George Kelly's work in the 1950s and 1960s verified and defined constructivist theory from a psychological perspective. As a clinical psychologist, he built his theory from extensive investigation of real people acting in a real world. Personal Construct Theory is the legacy he left in his insightful, provocative writings, in particular the classic *A Theory of Personality: the Psychology of Personal Constructs* (1963).[1]

Personal Construct Theory proposes that constructs are built out of a person's experience in order to anticipate future events. Constructs are the patterns that one formulates to make sense of the world. These patterns provide guidelines or frames of reference which determine the choices one makes. Individuals devise their own construct systems, which establish a personal orientation toward the events they encounter. Therefore, behavior is determined by the constructs one holds. It is highly individual rather than in response to stimuli as the behaviorist would explain. In Kelly's (1963) terms, "a person's processes are psychologically channelized by the ways in which he anticipates events" (p. 46).

Forming new constructs and reconstruing old ones are continual processes throughout life. All learning takes place this way. Underlying Personal Construct Theory is the endless opportunity for change. Kelly assures us that no one needs to paint himself or herself into a corner. We continue to learn throughout our lives. That is to

---

[1]Maher (1969) and Bannister (1977) compiled his other important papers after his untimely death.

say, we adjust our constructs to better match our environment and to improve our predictions upon which to base our actions. "All our present interpretations of the universe are subject to revision" (Kelly, 1963, p. 15).

The constructs that we have formed are not easily discarded, however. While we continually seek to improve these patterns, we are hampered by the damage to the system that results from alteration. Adjusting a construct may be a major psychological experience and entail considerable anxiety and threat.

Kelly (1963) describes the process of forming new constructs as progressing through a series of psychological phases. His descriptions of experience in the phases of construction are strikingly similar to Dewey's stages of reflective thinking. Actually, he was greatly influenced by Dewey's concept of reflective experience and built his psychological theory on Dewey's philosophical outlook. Kelly expanded on Dewey's model by emphasizing the disruption of new information to the person's system of constructs and the resulting increase in apprehension within the early phases of the process of construction. He found the threatening effect of the unknown to be a natural part of the constructive process.

## Phases of Construction – Interplay of Thinking and Feeling

Kelly (1963) classified common experience in constructing individual worlds as "a full cycle of sensemaking." While a person's constructs of the world are highly personal and individual, the process of construction has certain common features and characteristics that are experienced generally. Kelly elaborated on this basic premise of construct theory. The constructs that one builds are unique, but people experience the constructive process in certain common ways.

One of the major contributions of Kelly's work was his emphasis on the influence of feelings in the process of construction. He described the process of construction as naturally evolving through a series of phases and identified the predominant feelings commonly experienced in each phase.

A sequence of phases are commonly experienced in the process of constructing new information into one's system of personal constructs (see Table 2-2). When a person is initially confronted by a

Table 2-2.  Kelly — Five Phases of Construction

| PHASES | DEFINITION |
|---|---|
| Confusion and doubt | New experience |
| Mounting confusion and possible threat | Inconsistent/incompatible information |
| Tentative hypothesis | A direction to pursue |
| Testing and assessing | Assessing outcome of undertaking |
| Reconstructing | Assimilating new construct |

vague new idea, his or her system of constructs is either able to incorporate the idea or is inadequate to assimilate it. If the idea cannot be assimilated into the existing system of constructs, it is perplexing and one experiences confusion. Kelly asserts that "almost everything new starts with confusion" (Maher, 1969, p. 151). As individuals become more involved they find the new information is often inconsistent and incompatible with existing constructs; this increases their sense of confusion and uncertainty. The new experience may be so disruptive that the person becomes threatened by the prospect of the unknown. This brings us to a critical turning point in the process of construction. At that point, the individual may choose to reject the new idea. Kelly describes this phase as "the threshold between confusion and certainty, between anxiety and boredom . . . (when) we are most tempted to turn back" (Maher, 1969, p. 152). We have another choice, however. At this turning point, the person may choose to formulate a hypothesis to move the investigation of the idea toward assimilation.

By using the term, *hypothesis*, Kelly adopts the metaphor of a scientist whose ultimate aim is to predict and control. The hypothesis is a focus or a theme which gives a direction to pursue. Kelly asserts that a hypothesis can enable a person "to break through his moment of threat to get on with the task of testing to confirm or reject the hypothesis" (Maher, 1969, p. 151). The final phases of the cycle involve assessing the outcome of the undertaking and reconstruing or assimilating the new construct into the system (Bannister, 1977, pp. 14–15).

## Feeling and Formulating

Feelings interplay with thoughts and actions engaging the whole person in a complete experience of learning. Lack of consideration of any one of the three offers not only an incomplete but also an inaccurate picture. By directly addressing the impact of feelings on the process of construction, Kelly contributes the critical missing link for understanding the person's experience in any constructive process.

In Personal Construct Theory, hypothesis formulation plays an instrumental role as it does in Dewey's model of reflective thinking. Like Dewey, Kelly uses the term hypothesis not in its formal scientific sense but in a less structured psychological sense. Formulating is closely related to the feelings experienced within the constructive process. Formulating a "hypothesis" is a way to move beyond uncertainty and the associated, inhibiting feelings of confusion, doubt, and threat. Kelly offers a way of viewing a hypothesis and the instrumental part it plays in the process of construction. He describes two types of hypothesis statements, those in the invitational mood and those in the indicative mood (see Table 2–3) (Maher, 1969). A hypothesis stated in the invitational mood allows one to "suppose or behave as if the facts were known" (p. 149);

> An invitational hypothesis is not asserted as a fact but serves rather to make an unrealistic conclusion tenable for a sufficient period of time for a person to pursue its implications as if it were true. (p. 152)

The indicative mood, on the other side, has a prescriptive nature that dictates the direction to be taken.

The hypothesis establishes a frame of reference for the prediction of what is to follow. The invitational mood assumes the posture of expectancy and enables one to take risks and to profit from mistakes. The indicative mood limits the predictions that one can make and tends to close down or confine the task at hand. Both types of hypotheses move the process of construction from the initial state of confusion toward understanding. In information seeking, these moods may be envisioned either as styles and traits that are habitually

**Table 2–3. Two Types of Hypothesis Statements**

| MOOD (AFFECTIVE) | CHOICES (COGNITIVE) | ACTIONS (PHYSICAL) |
|---|---|---|
| Indicative | Predicting Closure | Confined to prescriptive task |
| Invitational | Predicting Expansion | Posture of expectancy for formulative task |

followed or as strategies and states that arise from a particular problem or stage of the process.

## Predicting and Choosing

Prediction plays an essential role in the constructivist theory of learning. Individuals form constructs with which to predict future events (Kelly, 1963, p. 14). Predictions lead to action which confirms or rejects the construct. We continually assess our constructs and reconstrue them to better match our world. The accuracy of our predictions determine the effectiveness of our actions. Through the reconstruction of constructs, predictions change and, as a result, behavior is altered.

Kelly (1963) describes the process of construction as a series of choices based on prediction of the outcome or result of the choice. He states that "a person chooses that which will extend and define his system" (p. 64). The choices that one makes are directed toward finding meaning and making sense of the world. Construction is a highly individual process based on one's system of prior personal constructs.

Kelly (1963) introduces the concept of elaborative choice that is a choice which broadens understanding (p. 65). Although all choices may hold this promise, choices that are truly elaborative change perspectives or provide clarification. Elaborative choices in the process of construction provide a pivotal point of greater understanding and clarity.

Although Kelly's explanation of prediction may seem overly systematic and structured, when he describes an individual's experience within the process of construction, a dynamic, uncertain process is revealed. When he depicts people working through the process by a series of choices from alternatives, these choices are anything but obvious and straightforward, particularly in the early phases.

## JEROME BRUNER: A CONTEMPORARY PERSPECTIVE

Bruner's research and writings are grounded in the earlier work of Dewey, Piaget (see Elkind, 1976), and Vygotsky (1978) as well as James, Goodman, and Bartlett. Three themes in Bruner's work

center on consideration of the nature of the: (1) knowledge, (2)
knower, and (3) knowledge-getting process. Although libraries have
traditionally attended to the first, we will concentrate here on the
latter two.

Bruner's studies of perception further verify and refine the constructive view of the nature of human thinking and learning. Bruner
was influenced by Frederick Bartlett's work as well as Piaget's
research on the concept of schema, which is similar to the notion of
construct. Bruner (1973) defined schema as:

> that integrated, organized representation of past behavior and expe-
> rience which guides individuals in reconstructing previously encoun-
> tered material which enables people to go beyond evidence, to fill in
> gaps, to extrapolate. (p. 5)

The constructive nature of thinking underlying schema theory has
provided the conceptual underpinnings for Bruner's study of a wide
variety of activities involving perception.

Bruner's (1973) research confirms that we are actively involved in
making sense of the world around us rather than being passive
receivers of information;

> The individual is seen not as a passive, indifferent organism but rather
> as one who actively selects information, forms hypotheses and on
> occasion distorts input in the service of reducing surprise and of
> attaining understanding. (p. 3)

This active process of learning is similar to that described earlier by
Dewey and Kelly. Bruner stresses our ability, indeed our compulsion,
to go beyond the information at hand to create a personal understanding. He describes perception as "an act of categorization which
is based on an inferential leap from cue to class identity and allows
us to go beyond the properties perceived to prediction" (p. 14). Like
Kelly, he sees the person interpreting or making sense of new
information in order to make more accurate predictions for action.

**The Interpretative Task**

Bruner's research and writing corroborates and elaborates on the
basic concepts in the constructive sequences of both Dewey and

Kelly. Bruner (1986) also describes construction as involving hypothesis generation which he views as a process of interpreting and creating. He notes that "We can create hypotheses that will accommodate virtually anything we encounter" (p. 51). Again, a hypothesis is not viewed in the strict scientific sense but as an imaginative story that allows us to "consider possible alternative personal perspectives on the world" (p. 54). The concept of choosing between possible alternatives corresponds to that of Kelly's work. Bruner suggests that we move along in the process of construction by suspending disbelief in order to consider possible worlds.

The interpretative task is central to the constructive process (see Table 2-4). It is not enough merely to gather information. Bruner (1986) explains that:

> If we are to understand it (new information), it will not be by means of a positivist archaeology in which everything particular about it and everything leading up to it are finally dug up, labeled, and collated. However much we dig and delve, there is still an interpretive task. (p. 53)

Interpreting involves creating. The interpretive task of "going beyond the information given" is a central concept in Bruner's work. Information is interpreted to create what Bruner calls products of mind. This mysterious capacity to interpret and create is at the core of what it means to be human. Bruner strives to understand the ways that human beings construct their worlds, and he wonders, "How we come to experience them as real, and how we manage to build them into the corpus of culture as science, literature, history, whatever" (Bruner, 1986, p. 45). The interpretive task is highly personal and is based on constructs built from past experience. This enables us to go beyond the information given to create something uniquely our own.

Table 2-4.  Bruner—The Interpretive Task

| PHASES | DEFINITION |
| --- | --- |
| Perception | Encountering new information |
| Selection | Recognizing patterns |
| Inference | Joining clusters and categories |
| Prediction | Going beyond the information given |
| Action | Creating products of the mind |

## Interplay of Thinking, Feeling, and Acting

The process of construction is not a systematic, orderly procedure, but rather it is the confusing, uncertain, threatening process that Kelly revealed. As Bruner (1986) cautions,

> I have rendered it all too gray and orderly. World making of this type rides from time to time on wild metaphors. . . . They are crutches to help us get up the abstract mountain. Once up, we throw them away (even hide them) in favor of a formal, logically consistent theory that (with luck) can be stated in mathematical terms. (p. 46)

Bruner decries the habit of drawing heavy conceptual boundaries around the classic triad: thought, action, and emotion. He warns of the misunderstanding that can result from making too sharp a distinction among the three;

> Emotion is not usefully isolated from the knowledge of the situation that arouses it. Cognition is not a form of pure knowing to which emotion is added and action is a final common path based on what one knows and feels. The three constitute a unified whole. (p. 117)

Bruner's work confirms Dewey's stages of reflective thinking and Kelly's phases of construction which incorporate feelings with thoughts and action. When we add the dynamic affective component to the constructive process, the full range of experience becomes apparent. Interpreting, choosing, and creating the inconsistent, often incompatible information encountered is likely to cause profound feelings of uncertainty, confusion, anxiety, and even threat. The critical impact of feelings in information seeking is illustrated by the conflict in any constructive process caused by encounters with unique or redundant information.

## Uniqueness and Redundancy

All new information is not treated equally in the constructive process of learning. There is a tension between the uniqueness and the redundancy of the information encountered within a new experience. Humans have a limited capacity for an overabundance of either the new or the familiar. This basic principle of human ability is important for understanding the interplay of affective experience with cognition and action in the process of construction.

Bruner's work reveals our inclination for seeking redundancy in new information. Our ability to recognize familiar patterns and to draw inferences leads to action. These familiar patterns are internal models or theories, similar to Kelly's constructs, which enable us to make predictions and to act (Bruner, 1986);

> Internal models or theories are built by redundancy, the ability to recognize similarity; inference, the ability to classify and categorize similarities, and generic coding systems, the mental models which allow one to go beyond the present by using probability and prediction. (p. 222)

As in Kelly's work, Bruner sees prediction or expectancy as an important component in recognizing redundancy. The basic principle of expectancy is revealed in his studies of perception. "Thresholds, the amount of time and input necessary for seeing or recognizing an object or event, are closely governed by expectancy. The more expected an event, the more easily it is seen or heard" (Bruner, 1986, p. 55). Too much familiarity, however, can cause attention to lag and lead to boredom.

Uniqueness, on the other hand, places our system on alert. Unexpected new information startles and surprises. There is a limit to the amount of unique information that the human system can take in. According to George Miller (1956), the capacity is $7 \pm 2$ slots, known as "the magic number." Bruner points out that you can get a lot of redundant, expected information into seven slots, but much less unique, unexpected information.

The notion of surprise explains the vigorous impact of uniqueness on the individual (Bruner, 1986);

> Surprise is a response to a violated presupposition. If what impinges on us conforms to expectancy, to the predicted state of the model, we may let our attention flag a little . . . Let input violate expectancy and the system is put on alert. (p. 46)

Kuhn's (1970) paradigm shift speaks to this problem. A paradigm shift incorporates a vast amount of unique information which startles, confuses, and disrupts.

We experience the tension between uniqueness and redundancy as the balance between anxiety and boredom. Our feelings play a critical role in motivating and directing our learning. Bruner refers to this as the affective threshold, which is explained in the *Yerkes-Dodson Law,* an established principle in psychology related to learning and motivation. The law states that (Bruner, 1986):

> The stronger the drive, up to a point, the faster learning will be. But beyond that point, increased drive will make an organism go out of control and will slow down learning . . . The effect of too much drive is to create a state that disrupts or otherwise interferes with effective cognition. (p. 111)

Bruner suggests that if we label this disruption "emotion" and use the concept to pursue the question of how cognition and emotion interact, the law suggests an economy of functioning based on a trade-off principle. "When need is high, the time given to information processing declines and the depth of that processing declines. Preoccupation with the goal smothers occupation with the means to it" (Bruner, 1986, p. 113). The concept of an affective threshold sheds light on the complex interplay of thoughts, actions, and feelings in the process of construction.

Learning is not a simple, straightforward cognitive process of assimilating new information. Affective experience of uncertainty and confusion complicate the process. Bruner (1986) finds "linkages between emotion, arousal, drive on the one side and learning, problem solving, thinking on the other. Such linkages bear upon the question of how we construct and construe the worlds in which we operate" (p. 113).

Let us consider the tension between uniqueness and redundancy within the constructive models of Dewey and Kelly (see Table 2-5). In the early phases when thoughts are vague and unfocused, the level of uniqueness would be expected to be high and redundancy low. At this point, it would be easy to exceed the affective threshold by introducing too much uniqueness. On the other hand, too much redundancy could result in lack of interest and boredom. The affective experience of the user is likely to have a profound effect on the process of construction.

Table 2-5.   The Constructive Process—Phases and Definitions

### Dewey—Phases of Reflective Thinking

| PHASES | DEFINITION |
|---|---|
| Suggestion | Doubt due to incomplete situation |
| Intellectualization | Conceptualizing the problem |
| Guiding Idea (hypothesis) | Tentative interpretation |
| Reasoning | Interpretation with more precise facts |
| Action | Idea tested by overt or imaginative action |

### Kelly—Five Phases of Construction

| PHASES | DEFINITION |
|---|---|
| Confusion and doubt | New experience |
| Mounting confusion and possible threat | Inconsistent/incompatible information |
| Tentative hypothesis | A direction to pursue |
| Testing and assessing | Assessing outcome of undertaking |
| Reconstructing | Assimilating new construct |

### Bruner—The Interpretive Tasks

| PHASES | DEFINITION |
|---|---|
| Perception | Encountering new information |
| Selection | Recognizing patterns |
| Inference | Joining clusters and categories |
| Prediction | Going beyond the information given |
| Action | Creating products of the mind |

## Summary of the Construction Process

These constructivists view learning as an active, engaging process in which all aspects of experience are called into play. We each construct our own personal worlds which may or may not agree with those of others around us. The process of construction is dynamic and driven by feelings interacting with thoughts and actions. People commonly experience the process of construction in a series of phases or stages with distinct changes in feelings, thoughts, and actions.

Personal Construct Theory describes the experience of individuals involved in the process of constructing meaning from the information they encounter. New information is assimilated in a series of phases beginning with confusion which increases as inconsistencies and incompatibilities are confronted within the information itself and between the information and the constructs presently held. As confusion mounts, it frequently causes doubt in the validity of the new information. The disruption caused by the new idea may become so threatening that the new information is discarded and the construction abandoned. At this point, however, another alternative is to form a hypothesis that can be tested and assessed in order to move toward incorporating the new construct into the existing system of personally held constructs. Forming a tentative hypothesis is the critical turning point in construing and reconstruing.

Taken together the theories of Dewey, Kelly, and Bruner provide a vivid explanation of construction. Affective experience plays a significant role in directing cognition and action throughout the process of construction. There is a delicate balance between uniqueness and redundancy in the information encountered as shown in Figure 2-1. An overwhelming intrusion of the new and unique may bring about feelings of uncertainty and anxiety on the one side. A profusion of redundancy causes disinterest and boredom on the other.

Thinking in the form of reflection is closely allied with acting throughout the process. Reflection leads to prediction which is a key component of construction. A prediction is an anticipation of an

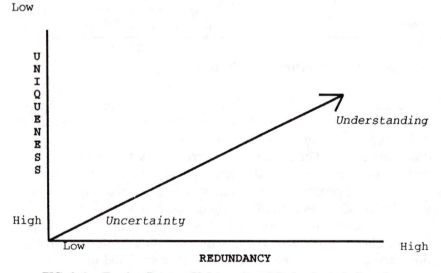

FIG. 2-1.  **Tension Between Uniqueness and Redundancy in Learning**

outcome. The process is driven by a desire to make accurate predictions. The choices that people make and the actions that they take are based on the predictions they make from the constructs they hold.

Reflection also leads to formulation, another critical component of the constructive process. A tentative predictive formulation, called a hypothesis by all three theorists, moves the individual out of uncertainty by providing a direction or a guiding idea, to borrow Dewey's term. Changes in feelings are associated with formulation bringing the three aspects of human experience into the constructive process. From a tentative formulation, individuals move beyond the information given to interpret and create something of their own. The process of construction incorporates a cycle of acting and reflecting, feeling and formulating, predicting and choosing, and interpreting and creating.

## KELLY'S PHASES OF CONSTRUCTION AND TAYLOR'S LEVEL OF INFORMATION NEED

By imposing Kelly's (1963) phases of construction on Taylor's (1968) levels of information need we can begin to visualize some elements of the constructive process, particularly the affective experience, that we may expect to observe in user's information seeking behavior (see Table 2-6). The Visceral level of need is an actual, but unexpressed, need for information which may be only a vague sort of dissatisfaction. The earliest phase of construction is characterized as a confusing, perplexing reaction to a vague new idea. The Conscious level of need is an ill-defined area of indecision which may be expressed in an ambiguous, rambling statement. Kelly describes the state of confusion and doubt as continuing to mount until the person may become

**Table 2-6. Comparison of Levels of Need and Phases of Construction**

| Taylor — Levels of Need | Kelly — Phases of Construction |
| --- | --- |
| Visceral — Q1 | Confusion and doubt |
| Conscious — Q2 | Mounting confusion and possible threat |
| Formal — Q3 | Hypothesis formulation |
| Compromised — Q4 | Testing, assessing, reconstruing |

quite threatened by the lack of understanding. At the level of Formal need the area of doubt may be described in concrete terms. Kelly states that a person can formulate a hypothesis enabling him or her to break through the moment of threat to get on with the task of investigating the new idea. At the Comprised level of need the person has translated his or her need into what the files can deliver in terms of the information system available. The final phases of construction are testing the hypothesis, assessing the results, and construing or reconstruing to assimilate the new idea. In this way, levels of information need may be thought of as a continuum within the process of construction.

After having summarized the borrowed theory and highlighted those aspects which seem particularly applicable to understanding the user's experience in information-seeking situations, the book discusses empirically testing the borrowed theory in information-seeking situations. The following three chapters describe a series of studies of library users in actual information-seeking situations. The data gathered from the participants in these studies were analysed within the frame of reference of the constructivist theory of learning summarized in this chapter. The findings of these studies provided the foundation for a grounded theory for library and information services articulated in the later chapters.

# Chapter 3

## The Information Search Process

Chapters 3–5 describe a series of five studies of library users in the process of seeking information for the completion of extensive projects. The studies were designed to observe people involved in information seeking over a period of time and to elicit their perceptions of what they are doing, thinking, and feeling in the process. Chapter 3 describes a small-scale qualitative study of high school seniors who were assigned research papers. A model of the information search process was developed from the common patterns which emerged within the context of the constructivist theory of learning. Chapter 4 describes two large-scale studies of library users to verify the model of the information search process. Chapter 5 describes further verification and expansion of the model in longitudinal studies of the same students who participated in the first study when they were at high school. Taken together these studies provide a basis for making the theoretical statement in the form of an uncertainty principle in Chapter 7 and further frameworks for designing practice in Chapters 8 and 9.

This research into the information search process grew out of three vantage points. First is the evidence in the literature of library and information science of the inadequacy of the bibliographic paradigm for addressing users' problems, as discussed in Chapter 1; second is an understanding of learning as a constructive process as it might be applied to learning from access to information contained in libraries as discussed in Chapter 2; and third is the author's direct, professional experience as a librarian.

Direct personal experience as a practitioner was a critical element in understanding the basic problem for study. Students in the daily course of seeking information for the completion of assignments were observed experiencing great difficulty regardless of the topic of the assignment or their ability level. Under the bibliographic paradigm they should have been able to proceed in a straightforward manner retrieving information from an organized collection of materials. Quite the contrary was the case. They were confused, anxious, and hurried, and frequently disinterested, annoyed, and frustrated. All of these are symptoms which any experienced teacher recognizes as potentially disruptive to the learning process. Why, after being given clear instructions on how to locate information and how to receive ample assistance in using sources as they proceeded, were students experiencing such negative feelings, particularly at the beginning of a project?

When these students' symptoms were placed within the context of the first and second vantage points, two basic questions occurred to this researcher. Is information seeking a process of construction in which students may expect to be confused and anxious? Is the bibliographic paradigm inadequate for mediation within the constructive process? Out of these speculations and reflections came the hypothesis that information seeking is a process of construction with all the accompanying dynamic complexities.

To investigate this hypothesis, the author applied exploratory methods to reveal the process for study and analysis. The initial study was a qualitative exploration of the search process of 25 academically capable high school seniors (Kuhlthau, 1985a, 1988a). Two research papers were assigned during the study, one each semester of the school year, in which students were given considerable latitude in selecting their topics. Instruments and methods (e.g., journals, search logs, short pieces of writing, and a questionnaire to elicit constructs related to information seeking in libraries) were developed to reveal aspects of the search process that would otherwise be hidden from an observer. In addition, case studies of six of the participants were conducted through a series of interviews, timelines, and flowcharts. Chapter 6 provides a complete description of the methods used in each of the five studies.

## PATTERNS IN THE CONSTRUCTIVE PROCESS OF
## INFORMATION SEEKING

Common patterns in the experience of this small, specialized group of library users were noted if they could be articulated and documented. While the pace of a search varied among individuals, certain aspects in the experience and the sequence remained relatively constant. Six stages in the search process were identified from the students' description of their experience; these stages match the phases in the process of construction. The following is a description of the patterns noted in students' experiences which are illustrated by some of their comments.

The *first stage* was task initiation. When the students received the assignment, they expressed feelings of uncertainty and apprehension. They needed to prepare for the decision of selecting a topic by understanding the assignment and relating it to prior experience. One student revealed that "When I first hear about an assignment, personally I just get upset." Another person described feeling "a spontaneous kind of fear." A student noted this to be a common experience among fellow students: "In the real beginning I guess I was like everyone else. I didn't know what I wanted to do . . . I felt anxious."

The uncertainty continued until a topic was selected; this was identified as the *second stage* of the process. If a topic was not chosen quickly, apprehension increased: "I felt anxious when I didn't have a topic. I was upset because even though I knew that the paper was due a long way off, everybody else seemed to be working and I wasn't," explained one student. When a topic had been selected, a sudden feeling of optimism was commonly expressed. "Once I have my topic I usually feel a great deal better and the idea of a research paper doesn't seem so cumbersome."

The *third stage* involved exploring information on the general topic in order to gain a focus. For many of the students this was the most difficult stage of the process. As they found information on their topics they frequently became confused by the inconsistency and incompatibility they encountered, which is the reaction the theory of construction would anticipate. One student declared, "I was so confused up until the 25th. I had no idea what direction I was going in." As another person recalled, "I felt kind of blind because I didn't know what I was looking for." A third student said "It seemed there was so much to do, it really scared me."

For some, the confusion became so threatening that they wanted to drop their topic at this point. "I went to look for a total change because I was really sick of it, the whole Elizabethan period. I had trouble with it; I was sick of it; I didn't want to do it anymore." The inclination to turn back and to abandon the quest at this point is also an expected reaction, according to the constructivist theory of learning.

Focus formulation is identified as the *fourth stage.* For many students this was the turning point in their research. The following example, from a student's journal, traces the thinking underlying focus formulation.

11/5: Decided to do a critical analysis of Mark Twain's Huck Finn.

11/8: Hope to find the theme that caused Huck Finn to be banned.

11/11: How Mark Twain's life in Mississippi affected his writings.

11/23: In the book were real events in Sam Clemens' life. I took great interest in the Colonel Sherburn chapters.

11/29: I am definitely doing Colonel Sherburn. [The next journal entry described her feelings.] OPTIMISM — I might be able to do this paper by Christmas.

The focus gave direction to the library search, and students expressed more confidence once they had reached this point: "I felt relieved: it makes things a lot easier once you have a basis for where you are going."

When students did not form a focus during the search process, they commonly experienced difficulty throughout the remainder of the assignment. One student elaborated on the difficulty that she had experienced:

I had a general idea not a specific focus, but an idea. As I was writing, I didn't know what my focus was. My teacher says she doesn't know what my focus was. I don't think I ever acquired a focus. It was an impossible paper to write. I would just sit there and say, "I'm stuck." There was no outline because there was nothing to complete. If I learned anything from that paper it is, you have to have a focus. You have to have something to center on. You can't just have a topic. You should have an idea when you start. I had a topic but I didn't know what I wanted to do with it. I figured that when I did my research it would focus in. But I didn't let it. I kept saying, "This is interesting and this is interesting and I'll just smush it all together." "It didn't work out."

A clear focus needed to be formed at this stage in the search process to enable students to progress to the next stage, as a hypothesis moves along a process of construction.

The *fifth stage* involved collecting information on the focus. Students described a sense of direction and feelings of confidence. As one student explained, "On December 9, I got my main focus. Before this I did basic research. After I got my focus, I got all of my sources to support the focus I had found." Another person declared that "After you know exactly what you are going to do it on, the research is easy."

Many students reported that their interest increased at this stage. As one student noted, "I sat down . . . and became totally interested in what I was reading." Another student added that "I didn't find this boring. I have senioritis and really didn't feel like doing it, but it was interesting what I found."

The *last stage* was the conclusion of the search process and the starting phase of the writing process. Students revealed different reasons for closing a search. Some ended when they encountered diminishing relevance: "You get what you want and then afterwards start getting off the topic a little." Another consideration was redundancy. "In the end you are just looking for extra things so you're sure you have everything. But it's a lot of repetition." Some concluded the search when they felt they had put forth sufficient effort. "After digging through five floors of books I said, "This is good enough. I've done a good enough job. The material I've gotten is sufficient." Students were aware of time constraints and closed the search near the date the assignment was due.

## AN EMERGING MODEL

The study proposed a new model for the process of information seeking encompassing the development of thoughts about a topic, the feelings that typically accompany such an evolution of thinking, and the actions of seeking and using sources. The task of each stage was categorized along with the feelings, thoughts, actions, and helpful strategies, as well as the mood found to be most productive.

The overall task was to form a perspective on the topic from the information encountered and to locate, interpret, and present information on the focused topic. Students' attempted to understand the task at the onset of the assignment, but they frequently concentrated on the mechanics, such as number of pages and sources, and the format of paper and citations rather than the intellectual task of selecting a topic and forming a focus for their search. This indication of a conflict related to task became a major finding in the later studies reported in Chapters 4 and 5.

Within the search process thoughts evolved from unclear, vague uncertainty to clearer, more focused understanding or in Belkin's (1980) terms from an anomalous state of knowledge to specificity. A series of phases or stages were evident as predicted by the models of construction (Kelly, 1963), of reflective thinking (Dewey, 1933), and of the interpretive task (Bruner, 1986). Information need emerged through levels as described by Taylor (1962, 1968).

An important finding was the sequence of feelings commonly experienced during the search. Students' feelings about themselves, the library, the task, and the topic evolved as their understanding of their topic deepened. The feelings that students described were predictable from Kelly's phases of construction. At the beginning of a search, evidence of uncertainty, confusion, and apprehension was isolated. Indications of increasing rather than decreasing uncertainty were noted as the search progressed. In the middle of the search evidence of a sense of clarity was documented as a focus was formed. With the focus, a sense of direction and confidence was common and that sense increased toward the end of the search.

As anticipated, the formulation of a focus was the turning point of students' feelings about their work. Before the focus was formed, they commonly felt confused and anxious. After the focus was formed, they felt more confident and had a sense of direction. In this way the focus served as an "elaborative choice" or a decision that advanced the process in a significant way. The focus served the same function as a hypothesis during the phases of construction — a step that a person takes to move out of the phase of confusion and on to the task of construing. The formulation of a focus provided a guiding idea or central theme which gave a direction to pursue around which the information seeking was centered.

The actions taken in the search also changed with the formulation of a focus. In the early stages students sought relevant information related to a general topic. After gaining the focus they sought pertinent information related to the focused topic. The concept of relevance and pertinence was adopted from Saracevic (1975). Relevance is a determination that information relates to or applies to the matter at hand, and has a connection or fits with the topic under investigation. Relevant information has some bearing upon the research topic and is considered useful in a search for information. Irrelevance is a determination that information does not fit or connect and does not contribute to understanding. Irrelevant information is outside of the boundaries of a topic and is considered not useful in a search for information.

Pertinence is a determination that information has a more decisive and significant relationship to a topic than relevance and is related to personal information need. Pertinent information is to the point and contributes to understanding or the solution of a problem. Pertinence is the determination that information is germane to the focus of a research topic and is considered most useful in a search for information.

## CRITERIA FOR MAKING DECISIONS

There were two major decision points during the search process: topic selection and focus formulation. Students use four criteria for making decisions about topic and focus: personal interest, assignment requirements, information available, and time allotted. They considered these criteria in terms of the perceptions that they held from former experience, and they predicted the outcome of each possible choice. Although their use of perceptions and prediction were not overt, when asked to explain their choices, they described reasoning based on the four criteria.

Personal interest arose from some familiarity with the topic, and interest increased after the search was well underway. Determining personal interest in a general topic at the beginning of a search appeared difficult. Students relied upon hunches and vague notions; "I read something about that once." "I saw something on TV." As constructs about the topic were formed during the search process, interest intensified. The issue of interest and intellectual engagement was critical to students' approaches to the search process.

Assignment requirements are the parameters set by the teacher. At the beginning, questions of mechanics — how much and in what form — often deflected the more intellectual questions leading to construction and personal learning.

The information available became a critical element in decisions of topic and focus. Students considered the convenience of using information at hand and often accommodated their choices accordingly. The limitation of one all-purpose, comprehensive search became apparent for meeting the information needs emerging in the process.

The time allotted was an important element throughout the search process but became a predominant factor in the later stages. Students made miscalculations about the amount of time needed for each stage of the process, usually underestimating the time required. They frequently used the negative term, "procrastination," to describe their sense of inaction during the early formative stages.

## STRATEGIES, EXPECTATIONS, AND ATTITUDES

A strategy is a tactic used to seek information or to work through a stage of the search process. Talking to a friend about a possible focus is a strategy, as well as consulting general sources before seeking specific materials. The strategies of talking, writing, and thinking seemed to be as important to students as the actual sources and formal search strategies that they used. Students used talking as a strategy to assist them in making decisions in their search process. Discussing the topic was an important strategy in the early stages of the process. They frequently involved informal mediators in this way.

A mediator is a person who intervenes in the search process of another. There are informal mediators, such as friends and family, and formal mediators, such as librarians and teachers. Formal mediators hold a professional position in which they are responsible for intervention, such as reference assistance or planned instruction. The study revealed a limited role for formal mediators; that role primarily centers around locating sources in the library collection. Several students expressed a desire for intervention in the process of their search and some frustration with the guidance received from formal mediators.

Students' expectations of the search process frequently did not match the process they were experiencing during the study. They did not expect to encounter uncertainty in the early stages and did not have a clear understanding of a sequence of tasks within the search process. The methods used to reveal the process for study helped students become aware of their own process and to discover that their experiences were common to other students. As one commented, "It helped to know that others were having trouble, too." Tolerating uncertainty and intentionally seeking a focus were strategies that students found to be particularly helpful in the process.

The attitude or mood found to be most productive for each stage was identified in the study. The terms, "invitational" and "indicative," were adopted from Kelly's personal construct theory. Invitational mood would foster an open search, one ready to take in new information. An indicative mood would foster an approach seeking closure. A mood indicates the way that a person approaches a task or event. The invitational mood leaves the person open to new ideas and receptive to change and adjustment according to what is encountered. In the indicative mood a person depends on the construct that he or she presently holds and rejects new information and ideas. The indicative mood directs the person toward closure and is the opposite of the invitational mood. An invitational mood is compatible with the early stages of the search process, and opens up extending strategies. Extension is a type of choice that leads to new information and ideas. An indicative mood was revealed as compatible with later stages of the search process leading to defining strategies. Definition is a type of choice that refines an existing idea.

## MODEL OF THE INFORMATION SEARCH PROCESS

The model of the information search process incorporates three realms: the affective (feelings), the cognitive (thoughts), and the physical (actions) common to each stage. The task considered most appropriate to move the process on to the subsequent stage is also included as well as some strategies that students used. Following is a description of the six stages of the search process as revealed in the findings of the initial study (see Figure 3-1).

**Stage 1: Task Initiation**

The first stage is Task Initiation when a person first recognizes that information will be needed to complete the assignment (see Table 3-1). When students, for example, first receive an assignment, they typically express feelings of uncertainty and apprehension. They think over the assignment in order to comprehend the task before them, to recall previous projects in which they have gathered information, and to identify possible alternative general topics. Actions frequently involve discussing possible topics and approaches.

**Stage 2: Topic Selection**

Feelings of uncertainty continue until the second stage of the process, or a general topic is selected (see Table 3-2). During Topic Selection, the task is to identify and select the general topic to be investigated or the approach to be pursued. Feelings of uncertainty often give way to optimism after the selection has been made, and there is a readiness to begin the search. Thoughts center on weighing perspective topics against the criteria of personal interest, assignment requirements, information available, and time allotted. The outcome of each possible choice is predicted, and the topic judged to have the greatest potential for success is selected. During this stage, actions may include making a preliminary search of information available, skimming and scanning for an overview of alternative topics, and talking to others about possibilities. When, for whatever reason, selection is delayed or postponed, feelings of anxiety are likely to intensify until the choice is made.

**Stage 3: Prefocus Exploration**

A third stage, Prefocus Exploration, is characterized by feelings of confusion, uncertainty, and doubt which frequently increase during

| Stages | Task Initiation | Topic Selection | Prefocus Exploration | Focus Formulation | Information Collection | Search Closure | Starting Writing |
|---|---|---|---|---|---|---|---|
| Feelings | uncertainty | optimism | confusion, frustration, and doubt | clarity | sense of direction/ confidence | relief | satisfaction or dissatisfaction |
| Thoughts | ambiguity ---------------------------------------------------→ increased interest ----------------------------------------→ specificity > | | | | | | |
| Actions | seeking relevant information ---------------------------------------------------------------→ seeking pertinent information | | | | | | |

**Figure 3-1. Model of the Information Search Process**

**Table 3-1. First Stage of the Search Process—Task Initiation**

| Task | Thoughts | Feelings | Actions | Strategies | Mood |
|------|----------|----------|---------|------------|------|
| **Stage 1 – Task Initiation** | | | | | |
| To prepare for the decision of selecting a topic | Contemplating assignment Comprehending Task Relating prior experience and learning Considering possible topics | Apprehension at work ahead Uncertainty | Talking with others Browsing library collection | Brainstorming Discussing Contemplating possible topics Tolerating uncertainty | Primarily Invitational |

**Table 3–2. Second Stage of the Search Process – Topic Selection**

| Task | Thoughts | Feelings | Actions | Strategies | Mood |
|------|----------|----------|---------|-----------|------|
| **Stage 2 – Topic Selection** | | | | | |
| To decide on topic for research | Weighing topics against criteria of personal interest, project requirements, information available, and time allotted<br>Predicting outcome of possible choices<br>Choosing topic with potential for success | Confusion<br>Sometimes Anxiety<br>Brief elation after selection<br>Anticipation of prospective task | Consulting with informal mediators<br>Making preliminary search of library<br>Using reference collection | Discussing possible topics<br>Predicting outcome of choices<br>Using general sources for overview of possible topics | Primarily Indicative |

this time (see Table 3-3). For many students, this is the most difficult stage in the process. The task is to investigate information on the general topic in order to extend personal understanding and to form a focus. Thoughts center on becoming oriented and sufficiently informed about the topic to form a focus or a personal point of view.

Information encountered rarely fits smoothly with previously held constructs, and information from different sources commonly seems inconsistent and incompatible. Users may find the situation quite discouraging and threatening, causing a sense of personal inadequacy as well as frustration with the system. Some actually may be inclined to abandon the search altogether at this stage. An inability to express precisely what information is needed makes communication between the user and the system awkward. Actions involve locating information about the general topic, reading to become informed, and relating new information to what is already known. Invitational strategies that open opportunities for extending constructs (e.g., listing facts that seem particularly pertinent and reflecting on engaging ideas), may be most helpful during this time. Strategies which foster an indicative rather than an invitational mood, such as taking detailed notes, may thwart the process by stressing premature closure.

**Stage 4: Focus Formulation**

Focus Formulation, the fourth stage, is for many the turning point of the search process when feelings of uncertainty diminish and confidence increases (see Table 3-4). The task is to form a focus from the information encountered. Thoughts involve identifying and selecting ideas in the information from which to form a focused perspective of the topic. The success of possible concentrations is predicted within the criteria of personal interest, assignment requirements, information available, and time allotted. Strategies for choosing a specific concentration within the general topic are reading over notes for themes and reflecting, talking, and writing about themes and ideas. The topic becomes more personalized during this stage if construction occurs. While a focus may be formed in a sudden moment of insight, it is more likely to emerge gradually as constructs become clearer. During this time, a change in feelings is commonly noted, with indications of increased confidence and a

**Table 3-3. Third Stage of the Search Process — Prefocus Exploration**

| Task | Thoughts | Feelings | Actions | Strategies | Mood |
|------|----------|----------|---------|------------|------|
| **Stage 3 — Prefocus Exploration** | | | | | |
| To investigate information with the intent of finding a focus | Becoming informed about general topic<br>Seeking focus in information on general topic<br>Identifying several possible focuses<br>Inability to express precise information needed | Confusion<br>Doubt<br>Sometimes threat<br>Uncertainty | Locating relevant information<br>Reading to become informed<br>Taking notes on facts and ideas<br>Making bibliographic citations | Reading to learn about topic<br>Tolerating inconsistency and incompatibility of information encountered<br>Intentionally seeking possible focuses<br>Listing descriptors | Primarily Invitational |

**Table 3-4. Fourth Stage of the Search Process — Focus Formulation**

| Task | Thoughts | Feelings | Actions | Strategies | Mood |
|------|----------|----------|---------|------------|------|
| **Stage 4 — Focus Formulation** | | | | | |
| To formulate a focus from the information encountered | Predicting outcome of possible foci<br>Using criteria of personal interest, requirements of assignment, availability of materials, and time allotted<br>Identifying ideas in information from which to formulate focus<br>Sometimes characterized by a sudden moment of insight | Optimism<br>Confidence in ability to complete task | Reading notes for themes | Making a survey of notes<br>Listing possible foci<br>Choosing a particular focus while discarding others or<br>Combining several themes to form one focus | Primarily Indicative |

sense of clarity. When individuals do not form a focus during the search process, they commonly experience difficulty throughout the remainder of the search, and when they begin to write or present findings. A clear focus enables a person to move on to the next stage, just as a hypothesis initiates testing in the process of construction.

## Stage 5: Information Collection

Information Collection is the fifth stage in the process when interaction between the user and the information system functions most effectively and efficiently (see Table 3–5). At this point, the task is to gather information pertaining to the focused topic. Thoughts center on defining and supporting the focus. Actions involve selecting information pertinent to the focus and taking detailed notes on that which pertains specifically to the focus as general information on the topic is no longer relevant after formulation. The user, with a clearer sense of direction, can specify the need for relevant, focused information to librarians and systems, thereby facilitating a comprehensive search of all available resources. Feelings of confidence continue to increase as uncertainty subsides with interest in the project deepening.

## Stage 6: Search Closure

In Search Closure, the last stage in the search process, feelings of relief are common. There is a sense of satisfaction if the search has gone well or disappointment if it has not (see Table 3–6). The task is to complete the search and to prepare to present or otherwise use the findings. Thoughts concentrate on culminating the search with a personalized synthesis of the topic or problem. Actions involve a summary search to recheck information that may have been initially overlooked. People reveal different reasons for closing a search. Some stop when they encounter diminishing relevance or evidence of redundancy, while others conclude the search when they feel they have put forth "sufficient" effort. Assuming a deadline, many people cease collecting information, not because they have exhausted the available sources, but because they need time to synthesize and prepare their final "product" before the due date. Organizing

Table 3-5. Fifth Stage of the Search Process – Information Collection

| Task | Thoughts | Feelings | Actions | Strategies | Mood |
|------|----------|----------|---------|------------|------|
| **Stage 5 – Information Collection** | | | | | |
| To gather information that defines, extends, and supports the focus | Seeking information to support focus Defining and extending focus through information Gathering pertinent information Organizing information in notes | Realization of extensive work to be done Confidence in ability to complete task Increased interest | Using library to collect pertinent information Requesting specific sources from librarian Taking detailed notes with bibliographic citations | Using descriptors to search out pertinent information Making comprehensive search of various types of materials, i.e., reference, periodicals, nonfiction, and biography Using indexes Requesting assistance of librarian | Combination of indicative and invitational |

**Table 3-6. Sixth Stage of the Search Process – Search Closure**

| Task | Thoughts | Feelings | Actions | Strategies | Mood |
|---|---|---|---|---|---|
| **Stage 6 – Search Closure** | | | | | |
| To conclude search for information | Identifying need for any additional information<br>Considering time limit<br>Diminishing relevance<br>Increasing redundancy<br>Exhausting resources | Sense of relief<br>Sometimes satisfaction<br>Sometimes disappointment | Rechecking sources for information initially overlooked<br>Confirming information and bibliographic citations | Returning to library to make summary search<br>Keeping books until completion of writing to recheck information | Indicative |

strategies, such as outlining, for preparing to present or otherwise using the information are applied.

The results of the initial study of the small sample of library users suggested that affective symptoms associated with construct building may be a natural part of the information search process and commonly experienced by users. This study provided a window into the user's experience within the search process and offered an indepth description of a new problem by providing many layers of data collected over an extended period of time for the purpose of developing a grounded theory. The research hypotheses and process model generated in this study required testing using quantitative methods on a larger, more diverse sample of library users in different information environments in order to validate and generalize the findings.

## SUMMARY OF MAJOR FINDINGS

This chapter has presented a model of information seeking derived from an intensive study of a group of high school seniors. The model describes the information search process from the user's perspective as being experienced in six stages of thoughts, feelings, and actions. The model is presented in two forms; Figure 3–1, which depicts the entire process from initiation to closure, and Tables 3–1 to 3–6, which describe each stage in the process. In the tables, the task most appropriate to move the process along is identified for each stage, as well as thoughts, feelings, actions, strategies, and mood.

The major finding in this study is that the patterns of experience of these information users matched those described in the process of construction. The main contribution is the articulation of information seeking as a process of construction in the form of a model.

Several problems related to information provision began to surface in this study. One is a conflict between students' understanding of their task in information seeking and their actual experience in the process of information seeking. Their expectations of the process and the task did not match their experience. Uncertainty and the more formulative task of the early stages were frequently met with impatience and a sense of inadequacy. An expectation of uncertainty at the beginning of the process was needed for tolerating uncertainty and assuming the task of intentionally seeking a focus to guide the search. An additional problem is students' limited perception of librarians as merely locators of sources. Such a perception was inadequate to mediate in the dynamic process of the search.

The model of the information search process needed to be verified in a larger more diverse sample of library users. The next chapter describes two large-scale studies to validate the model.

# Chapter 4

## Verification of the Model of the Information Search Process

The results of the initial study of the small sample of library users, as described in Chapter 3, suggested that thoughts and feelings associated with construct building may be commonly experienced by users in the information-search process. The research hypothesis and process model, however, required further study in order to validate and generalize the model. Two studies were conducted using quantitative methods on a larger, more diverse sample of library users in different information environments.

The model of the Information Search Process depicts information seeking as occurring in six stages with patterns of thoughts, feelings, and actions commonly experienced by user's involved in extensive information problems. The general research question for further verification was: Does the model of the information search process hold for a large, diverse sample of library users? The model was based on the finding that uncertainty, a natural and necessary aspect of the early stages of the search process, causes discomfort and anxiety which, in turn, affect articulation of a problem, choices made within a search, and actions taken toward addressing an information need.

### STUDY OF THE SEARCH PROCESS OF A LARGER SAMPLE OF HIGH SCHOOL SENIORS

The model which had been developed in a small sample of academically competent high school library users was tested in a larger sample of more academically diverse high school students. The study examined the information search process of high-, middle-, and low-achieving high school seniors (Kuhlthau, 1989) to verify the model. Three questions were addressed, two related to verifying the model and the other investigating a further issue of outcome or relation of process to product. Do other high achievers experience a process similar to those in the initial sample? Do low and middle level students experience a similar process? Does the search process relate to the teacher's assessment of the product?

Participants were 147 seniors, in English classes in six high schools, who were identified as high, average, and low achievers. A research paper assignment of four weeks' duration was made. Process surveys were administered at three points in the search process, Initiation, Midpoint, and Closure, eliciting thoughts and feelings at each point; see Chapter 6 for a complete description of the study. Teachers assessed the students' papers for presence of focus, quantity of sources, and normal grading. The data from 40 participants identified as low achievers were incomplete and could not be analyzed in the study. There was no significant difference, however, between the high and middle achievers, with the exception of grade; the high achievers received higher grades.

High and middle achieving high school participants showed a significant change in thoughts, during completion of the search process, moving from general background, to specific and more narrowed, to clearer and more focused. There was a similar significant difference in their confidence and feelings during the process, with confidence increasing throughout and feelings moving from confused to confident and relieved.

Participants' thoughts changed during the search process from general and background at Initiation with a mean of 5.89, to specific and narrowed at Midpoint with a mean of 7.20, to clearer and focused at Closure with a mean of 8.52. A single-tailed t-test showed significant differences in means from Initiation to Midpoint and Midpoint to Closure at $p < .001$. In a similar way, students' feelings changed during the search process. At Initiation they reported a mean confidence level at 5.37, which increased only slightly at Midpoint to 5.70, but increased significantly at Closure to 6.83. While the change is not as pronounced as that of thoughts, there was a substantial gain in the confidence of the students from Initiation to

Closure. Figure 4–1 shows that the change in thoughts parallels a rise in confidence from Initiation to Midpoint to Closure, during the search process.

## RELATION OF CHANGES IN CONFIDENCE AND OUTCOME OF SEARCH

There was some evidence of relationship between changes in feelings during the search process and the outcome of the search. Slight correlation was noted between increase in confidence and the teachers' assessment of focus in the papers, and the grade on the papers. There was, however, no correlation between increased confidence and the quality and variety of the sources used in the papers. According to the model, an increase in confidence corresponds to an increase in clarity and focus in thoughts, and may also correspond to evidence of construction. Correlation between increased confidence and the quality of student papers indicates that there may be a connection between process and outcome, an important issue which warrants further investigation. On the other hand, within the context of the model of the search process, the quality and variety of sources used may not necessarily indicate construction, i.e., clarification of thoughts. Lack of correlation between the students' use of sources and the teachers' assessment of

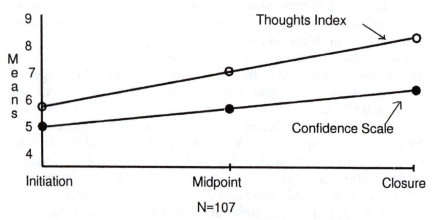

FIG. 4–1.   **Change in Thoughts and Confidence in Search Process**

focus in their papers, although not surprising within the context of this research, does not support the traditional view of information use within the bibliographic paradigm.

These findings verify the model of the search process with high- and middle-level seniors. Information seeking is a complex learning process which involves finding meaning. Thoughts evolve, feelings change, and confidence rises as a search progresses.

## MAJOR FINDINGS AND IMPLICATIONS

The main finding of this study of high school seniors is that the information seeking of college-bound students developed as a process over time in which thoughts evolved and feelings of confidence increased. The underlying concept of the model of the information-search process was verified in this study, thereby revealing a process of learning that began with vague thoughts and low confidence and closed with significant clarification of thoughts and increased confidence.

A major disappointment was the inability to collect sufficient data for analysis from the lower-level students. The design of the study required that participants complete surveys at three specific points. High incidence of absenteeism caused these students to miss many of the critical days on which data were collected. Most of them simply were not in school on one of the three days designated for data collection. (Another study using flexible tracking methods and perhaps a more qualitative approach is required to investigate the search process of this population.)

An interesting aspect of the findings was an indication of some correspondence between the process that the students had experienced and the product of their search. A correlation was found, albeit a slight one, between the student's increase in confidence during the search process and the teacher's assessment of focus in their papers. This is the only study in this series to address the outcome of the search. The quality of the outcome or the product of the search is a key issue in our concern with mediation. Ultimately, we need to address the effectiveness of mediation in terms of the outcome of the search. The outcome of the information search process is learning. However, the number of sources did not correlate with the teacher's assessment of focus in the students' papers. This suggests that the quality of the process has more impact on learning than does the quality of sources. Therefore, mediation in the bibliographic paradigm of locating sources is likely to be inadequate to address the process of learning from information.

## STUDY OF THE SEARCH PROCESS OF ACADEMIC, PUBLIC, AND SCHOOL LIBRARY USERS

Another study in this series addressed the problem of validating the model of the search process among a wider sample of library users. Up to this point, the research had centered on studies in school libraries and had not addressed the question of whether there were similar patterns in the process of other users and in other types of libraries. Further testing of the model was conducted with 385 academic, public, and school library users in 21 sites (Kuhlthau, Turock, George, and Belvin, 1990).[1]

Findings revealed a similar process across types of library users, with participants seeking background information at Initiation and information related to the general topic at Midpoint and Closure, with some seeking information on a focused perspective of the topic at closure. Descriptions of thoughts were general and vague at Initiation, narrowed and clearer at Midpoint, with 50 percent of the users making focused statements of their perspective of the topic at Closure. Confidence increased significantly from Initiation to Closure. The adjectives most used to describe feelings were confused, frustrated, and doubtful at Initiation and satisfied, sure, and relieved at Closure.

The first three questions on the survey elicited cognitive aspects of the search process (see Table 4-1). Responses indicated that thoughts about the topic became clearer and more focused as respondents moved through the search process seeking more pertinent and focused information. Although there was strong evidence of clearer thinking about a topic as a search progressed, many participants did not make a focused statement at all during the search process.

---

[1]This study was funded by the US Department of Education through a Library Research and Demonstration Grant.

Table 4–1.   Evidence of Cognitive Aspects

**"What are you looking for?"**
**Response Percentage**

| N = | Initiation 363 | Midpoint 312 | Closure 316 |
|---|---|---|---|
| Background | 81 | 19 | 4 |
| Relevant | 9 | 70 | 17 |
| Focused | . | 4 | 25 |
| Other | 10 | 7 | 54 |

**"Describe the topic in a short paragraph."**
**Response Percentage**

| N = | Initiation 341 | Midpoint 312 | Closure 314 |
|---|---|---|---|
| General | 71 | 11 | 5 |
| Narrowed | 23 | 80 | 45 |
| Focused | . 2 | 9. | 50 |
| Other | 4. | | |

**"What is the title of your project?"**
**Response Percentage**

| N = | Initiation 336 | Midpoint 305 | Closure 315 |
|---|---|---|---|
| No Title Yet | 32 | 18 | 13 |
| Vague | 48 | 29 | 25 |
| Clearer | 18 | 42 | 36 |
| Compromised | . 2 | 12 | 26 |

The fourth question sought to reveal those who were perceived as mediators during the search process (see Table 4-2). Responses indicated that 39 percent of the respondents consulted experts, 25 percent conferred with librarians, 20 percent reported conferring with friends and family, and 13 percent talked with peers. There was no significant change from Initiation to Midpoint to Closure, nor was there a significant difference by type of library.

The next question addressed the affective aspects of the search process (see Table 4-3). Responses revealed confidence steadily increasing with lowest confidence at Initiation, confidence rising significantly at Midpoint, and with another significant increase at Closure.

Question 6, which further addressed the affective elements in the

Table 4-2.  Evidence of Role of Mediators

**"Who have you talked to about your project?"**
Response Percentage

| N = | Initiation 348 | Midpoint 305 | Closure 315 |
|---|---|---|---|
| No One | 15 | 8 | 7 |
| Family/Friends | 15 | 17 | 20 |
| Peer | 12 | 12 | 13 |
| Expert | 39 | 38 | 38 |
| Librarian | 19 | 25 | 22 |

Table 4-3.  Identification of Confidence Level

**"On the scale below indicate your confidence level at this point in the project."**
Percentage Frequency

| N = | Initiation 361 | Midpoint 313 | Closure 329 |
|---|---|---|---|
| 1 Low | 4 | 2 | 1 |
| 2 | 5 | 3 | 1 |
| 3 | 10 | 4 | 2 |
| 4 | 12 | 8 | 4 |
| 5 | 14 | 16 | 10 |
| 6 | 9 | 14 | 9 |
| 7 | 16 | 19 | 15 |
| 8 | 15 | 19 | 23 |
| 9 | 7 | 9 | 26 |
| 10 High | 7 | 6 | 12 |
| Mean | 5.8 | 6.5 | 7.6 |

search process, listed 10 adjectives, taken from the model, from which respondents were asked to select in order to describe their feelings at Initiation, Midpoint, and Closure. The feelings checked by the participants matched those predicted in the model. There was a significant difference between Initiation and Closure for all adjectives. Confidence increased from Initiation to Closure, as did the responses "satisfied," "sure," and "relieved." Responses of "confused," "frustrated," and "doubtful" decreased from Initiation to Closure. "Optimistic," was a consistently high selection at each point for participants in all three types of libraries.

In summary, the findings indicate that participants' thoughts about their topics became clearer and more focused as they moved through the search process seeking more relevant and focused information. Feelings accompanying the changes in thoughts matched those predicted in the model, with confidence steadily increasing. Uncertainty, confusion, and frustration decreased during the process as feelings of being satisfied, sure and relieved increased.

## DIFFERENCES AMONG THE GROUPS STUDIED

There were, however, some differences among the groups of library users studied. Comparison of users in three types of libraries revealed some differences in the levels of confidence reported as they progressed through the stages of the search process. The public library users were more confident at Initiation than were the academic and school participants. While the academic and school library users indicated similar levels of low confidence at Initiation, the college students were significantly more confident at Closure than were the high school students.

### Perception of Task

An important finding in the study of three types of library users was that while participants' thoughts and feelings matched the model as anticipated, their identification of task did not (see Table 4–4). The tasks predicted by the model show a progression from recognizing an

Table 4-4. Comparison of Tasks in the Information Search Process (ISP)

| Stages in ISP | Appropriate Task According to Kuhlthau Model | Task as Reported by Study Participants |
|---|---|---|
| Initiation | Recognize Information Need | Gather |
| Selection | Identify General Topic | Gather |
| Exploration | Investigate Information on General Topic | Gather/Complete |
| Formulation | Formulate Focus | Gather/Complete |
| Collection | Gather Information Pertaining to Focus | Complete |
| Presentation | Complete Information Search | Write or Present |

information need, to identifying a general topic, to exploring information on a general topic, to formulating a specific focus, to gathering information pertaining to the specific focus, and to completing the information search. Most participants limited their responses to the tasks of gathering and completing in all stages; few, however, selected the more formative tasks at any point in the process. While gathering and completing are traditional information-seeking tasks, exploring and formulating may be more compatible with thoughts and feelings commonly experienced in the early stages of the information search process.

**Focused Perspective**

In addition, half of the users in academic, public, and secondary school libraries studied did not show evidence of reaching a focused perspective of their topic at any time during the search process. Although a significant change in thoughts was found, only 50 percent of the participants made focused statements of their topic at the close of their search. Furthermore, while most participants were seeking background information at Initiation and information relevant to the general topic at Midpoint, at Closure only 25 percent reported that they were seeking information on a focused perspective of the topic. These findings lead to the assumption that many people may have entered the presentation or writing phase without clearly, focused topics.

For some people, organizing and writing in preparation for presenting may enable them to focus their thoughts. The result is that formulation occurs at a later point in the process than indicated in the model. On the other hand, lack of a personal perspective may be the result of the notion that the purpose of a search is to reproduce an author's view rather than to make sense within one's own frame of reference, a perception which may inhibit the process of construction during the search process.

## MAJOR FINDINGS AND IMPLICATIONS

The major finding in this study was that the model of the information search process held for library users in academic and public libraries as well as with a range of high school students. The high school sample were selected from students in grades 10 through 12 across subject areas. Further testing is needed, however, in even more diverse groups, particularly in academic and public libraries and with lower-achieving high school students. As the academic participants were limited to undergraduates, the study did not reveal whether graduate students and faculty experience a similar constructive process in information use. Further research is also needed with public library users and with the population of potential library users. While this work provides a good beginning for research into the constructive process of information seeking, further investigation into the experience and process of novice and expert information users with diverse information problems is needed.

To summarize the findings of this series of studies on the user's perspective of the search process, the affective symptoms of uncertainty, confusion, and frustration prevalent in the early stages were associated with vague, unclear thoughts about a topic or problem. As the participant's knowledge state shifted to clearer, more focused thoughts, a corresponding shift was noted in feelings of increased confidence and certainty. Satisfaction and relief are common at the conclusion of the search process.

Some implications for mediation in different types of libraries are suggested. The low level of confidence of students, both in high school and in college, at the beginning of assignments indicates the need for guidance in the process of searching and support in the early stages of learning from gaining access to information. The higher level of confidence of the public library participants may indicate the competence of more experienced, expert library users. Further study may uncover less competent novice public library users who need similar process intervention early on.

A clear problem emerges from this study which also was indicated in the studies of high school students. Users perceive the task of the search process as primarily to gather information even in the early stages of vague, unfocused thinking. Users do not clearly understand the task of forming a focused perspective from the information encountered in the early stages of the search process. Users need guidance and counseling in the task most appropriate for moving on to the next stage. A role for information professionals in the search process is indicated beyond that of locating sources. A new kind of intervention that meets the process needs of information users is indicated.

# Chapter 5

## Longitudinal Confirmation of the Information Search Process

As we have seen, a constructive process takes place over an extended period of time and cannot be studied within the framework of a single incident. In the initial model-building study and the large-scale validation studies, discussed in the previous chapters, the changes that accompany the process of learning from information were examined over a period of 1 month to 1 year. In this sense, each of the studies in this series have been longitudinal. Two further studies, however, were extended over a period of 5 years applying the longitudinal approach as a method of data collection for comparison.

The theory of construction proposes that the way we view the world is based on the constructs we build from our personal experience. Therefore, the experiences that we have related to information use determine the way that we perceive the information-seeking process. We cannot fully know what perceptions have been formed in a particular experience until some time later when that experience has become an integral part of our system of constructs and the way that we view the world. Therefore, longitudinal studies are essential for revealing the constructs that individuals have built over time. Two such longitudinal studies of the panel of students in the original study were conducted.

Full reports of these studies have been published previously. This chapter discusses those critical elements revealing information seeking as a process of construction.

## PERCEPTIONS OF INFORMATION SEEKING AFTER
## FIVE YEARS

One of the longitudinal studies addressed the problem of how students' perceptions of the search process had changed after four years of college and how their perceptions compared with the six stages of the model (Kuhlthau, 1988b). The same questionnaire eliciting perceptions, which had been administered to this group in high school, was used to provide longitudinal data on their perceptions, with 20 of the original 25 students responding. Although the term, "perceptions," was used rather than "constructs," for all intents and purposes, the working definition would be the same for both terms within this research. Responses after college were compared with those that they gave in high school, and statistically significant changes were determined.

Comparison of the panel of participants when they were in high school and after four years of college revealed certain perceptions of more experienced information users. The study showed that the model held over time for this select group of students.

The students' perceptions of information search activity changed during the four years of college in several ways. Significant changes were found in 3 of the 6 areas studied: research assignments, focus formulation, and procedures for gathering information. Perceptions pertaining to research assignments revealed that interest in a topic increases as a search progresses. Perceptions pertaining to focus formulation revealed that a topic changes as information is gathered and that a central theme evolves as information is gathered. Perceptions pertaining to procedures for gathering information showed a decreased emphasis on the card catalog as the only place to initiate a search and increased emphasis on the use of periodicals.

Perceptions of research assignments shifted significantly in two important respects. First in college, the students were found to expect to become more interested in a topic as they learned more about it in the process of a library search. As the model describes, interest increases as a search progresses. The expectation of deepening interest provides the motivation for pushing on through the confusing, frustrating prefocus stage. Another perception that students held related to assignments that changed during the four years of college. That perception was that a library assignment adds to what is learned in a course. The students came to perceive library use as related to course work rather than an extraneous requirement. When students realize that using information in the library extends and deepens their course learning, research assignments are attributed greater validity and purpose.

Perceptions of formulating a focus within a topic also changed during college years to match the model more closely. According to the model, focus formulation is the pivotal point in the search process, the point at which the user moves out of confusion and doubt and on to clarity and purpose. In college, the students came to expect a topic to change during a search for information. They also came to expect a central theme to evolve during a search for information. These perceptions enable users to be open to learning from the ideas that they encounter in a library search and to avoid seeking only that information that supports their preconceived notions of a topic. Some change was also noted in the perceptions of the students toward changing a topic according to the availability of materials.

There was no significant change in the perceptions in the other three areas—general library use, topic selection, and role of mediators. These students perceive themselves as library users in high school and continue this view through college. There was a slight change noted in the use of more than one library. Fewer students reported the use of more than one library when they were in college than when they were in high school, which can be explained by the common practice of using both the high school media center and the public library whereas at college they tended to use only the campus library. Although there was a slight gain in their preference for topics that they chose themselves over those suggested by the teacher, this was not statistically significant.

Although there was no significant change in the role of mediators, this area warrants some further comment. While the students perceived a minimal role for teachers and librarians, they disclosed that they talk to others about their topic. In high school 62 percent, and in college 80 percent, of the students responded that they "almost always" or "often" talk to others about their topic. In the questions related to their perceptions about seeking help from librarians or teachers, however, most of their responses fell into the "sometimes," "seldom," or "almost never" categories. The perception of a need to talk about their topic did not alter their perception of a minimal role for formal mediators, such as librarians and teachers.

## LONGITUDINAL CASE STUDIES

A longitudinal study also was conducted of the case study participants to offer fuller description of changes in perceptions of the search process over time (Kuhlthau, 1988c). Four of the 6 original case study subjects were interviewed, in one-hour sessions, after completion of 4 years of undergraduate education.

The perceptions of each of the case study participants were analyzed under the following five categories: research assignments, topic selection, search process, procedures for gathering information, and role of mediators.

### Research Assignments

All 4 participants had positive attitudes toward research assignments and saw themselves as scholars who would be using libraries for this type of work in the future. J had the concept of contributing to the literature of a field and explained that in one assignment he had to "put (his) work back into the literature." Participants preferred research papers over other types of course requirements, namely exams and multiple-choice tests. For C, research assignments were actually a preferred way of learning. "I have better control of my grade and I learn a lot more. I remember more from those research papers I did than I did from any of the classes I have ever taken." Another stated that, "for me, going into science and trying to get a Ph.D., writing a paper is a very important skill . . . I am happy when I am given an opportunity to do a paper that a person will read and criticize."

Each of the students noted feelings of uncertainty and confusion which remained prevalent in the early stages of completing research assignments. C had come to expect to be confused at the beginning of a search and had learned not to "panic." Another student explained that she "puts off going to the library but that she is not as bad about this as are some people." Another person explained how she had come to tolerate her feelings at the beginning by understanding the whole process. "I used to be very anxious. But now I know how to go about it. I don't get upset anymore. I know it will take $x$ amount of time to do the research, to narrow down my topic, and to begin writing. I know how I work."

**Topic Selection**

When selecting a topic each of the students attempted to internalize the assignment and create his or her own personally felt information need. They preferred to choose their own topics rather than being given a topic "out of a hat" or "by a lottery." When given the opportunity, they designed topics which were meaningful to them, and ones with which they had some familiarity or a particular interest. All 4 students built on topics from prior research papers they had done. While this may have been an attempt to make the task easier, it also indicated identification of an area of specialization and movement toward developing expertise in certain subjects. As students matured and had more experience with conducting library research, they sought to mold an assignment to their own area of interest and concern.

Many of the topics that the students chose for research papers related to the careers for which they were preparing. One economics major explained that he chose topics that

> weren't even on the list of one hundred possible topics that the professor gave out. Those were ideas that I had in the back of my mind that I had researched to a lesser degree and had touched on in other classes. Both dealt with the economic development of Mexico. Actually one was a continuation of the other.

A premed student who was enrolled in an engineering course explained how she accommodated a topic to her interest. In a Civil Engineering course on structures,

> We had to do a structural analysis of something . . . I was trying to think of an interesting building. People were doing the Astrodome, the Brooklyn Bridge, the Coliseum, the Pantheon. It just came to me that the skeleton would be interesting. The elbow is a basic hinge joint and the hip, a ball and socket.

Choosing a topic involves a tension between alternative approaches. On the one hand, there is the opportunity for building repertoire and expanding knowledge. On the other, there is the inclination to play it safe, set up success, and conserve energy. Habitual approaches which remained consistent over time were evident in the subjects' explanations of how they selected topics. The criteria of personal interest, assignment requirements, information available, and time allotted were applied for making choices as the model revealed. Personal interest, however, was attributed greater importance than in the earlier case study. As the student who chose the skeleton as a structure explained,

> I was very excited about the topic. When I had a hard time finding information I didn't want to change it. There was nothing else I wanted to do. It turned out to be a really fun paper to write. I got some pictures and sketches. I had to get materials on interlibrary loan.

## Search Process

All 4 participants saw the search process as taking place over a period of time for which they had to plan in advance. Each had a concept of the amount of time needed for searching. However, perceptions of time differed and may have been based on preferred ways of learning generally. There was a marked difference between one student's approach to searching taking place over a 4- or 5-day span and another's approach, extending over 4 to 6 weeks.

They used metaphors to describe a purposeful, sensemaking process in which they were actively seeking to increase their understanding of the problem or topic before them. One person sought "a story out of the whole thing" and another "a thread for tieing the parts together. I look for a main string that runs through all of the sections." Another participant described seeking to answer all of her questions, and one of the student explained that this "focusing and narrowing were the most difficult part of the search."

Searching was not described as a strictly linear process. Both D and C explained how they worked their way through the literature interspersing use of indexes and catalogs with browsing and following leads which opened up along the way. While students perceived the process as moving from general information to specific, their descriptions of searching revealed more of a spiral of thoughts building through the information encountered rather than a neat step-by-step progression.

Frequently one source that was particularly relevant to a topic was found late in the search;

> There was one book which went through everything. That was my major source of information. That came kind of late. But it was ok because (from) the information I had gotten previously I was already familiar enough with what I wanted to concentrate on.

The "one critical source" is recognized as pertinent after considerable formulation has taken place.

By the way, one of the most noted changes in the case study participants' use of sources was that recent materials which were not considered particularly important in high school were regarded as essential in college.

Students had personalized their determinations of closure and concept of what is enough. A search was considered completed by G and C when they had exhausted all sources. D described having an internal feeling that she had everything. J sought to find a "story" rather than to exhaust all sources. He stated that if he had wanted he could have uncovered most of the sources on a topic. However, comprehensiveness did not seem necessary to him.

## Procedures for Gathering Information

Each participant had developed a system for gathering and organizing information which he or she described as his or her own personal way of approaching the research task. The students' systems, however, had marked similarities. They took few notes at the beginning of a search, and all used yellow pads. C was the only one to use notecards and his use was limited to recording major points. J reported that he took no notes but, instead, underlined photocopied texts. All participants used outlining to organize for writing; they did this toward the close of the search. They developed similar methods of coding notes and articles by using symbols, such as stars, checks, and different colors.

All of the subjects were confident in their own searching ability, with G and C appearing the most confident and D and J seeming somewhat less confident. D expressed some fear of not measuring up to past performances. J allowed less time than the others to gather, organize, and write papers, and frequently expressed dissatisfaction with the final outcome.

## Role of Mediators

Participants mentioned three types of mediators: professors, librarians, and other students. While all 4 did use mediators to some extent, librarians played a minimal role in their search process. C and G conferred with professors and other students quite extensively. G had worked successfully on group projects with other students. Librarians were expected to answer location questions and little else; they were not expected to have sufficient subject expertise to recommend sources. Instruction given by librarians was described as inadequate and not tailored to the students' majors. Further discussion revealed dissatisfaction with the role that librarians had played. D pointed out that although librarians were available, students have to go to them; they do not come to the students, and some students are reluctant to reveal their ignorance by asking a question. C noted that students need help with the process of a search. Both C and D had assumed the role of mediator for fellow students. J sought independence and remained isolated in his process for the most part. All were dissatisfied with librarians as mediators, to some degree, and expressed the need for increased participation and a more proactive role for librarians.

## SUMMARY OF CASE STUDY PERSPECTIVE

Examination of the case study participants reveals an understanding of the search process and a tolerance for the ambiguity and uncertainty of the earlier stages. They had gained a sense of their own pace in the information search process, expected to be uncertain at the beginning, and had developed tolerance for the early uncertainties in the formative stages. They also showed a sense of ownership in the process and the strategies that they used to work through the stages, referring to "my process" and relating "this is the way I do it." While they described experiencing a sequence of stages, they related a somewhat recursive, iterative process in which they moved toward a clearer, focused perspective rather than one that was strictly linear.

For these users, the information search process had become an important way to learn rather than just a means for fulfilling requirements for a course. They showed an awareness of being involved in seeking meaning by purposefully engaging in "focusing and narrowing," and in seeking "a thread," "a story," and "answers to all my questions." Discussion of the topics that they chose for research assignments showed evidence of molding an imposed task to their own interests, building on prior searches, and developing areas of expertise.

## VERIFICATION AND EXPANSION OF THE MODEL OF THE SEARCH PROCESS FROM LONGITUDINAL STUDIES

Analysis of the two longitudinal studies showed that the participants experienced stages similar to those identified in the original model of the search process. While the process appears to be accurately described, the data also indicated several areas in which the original model may be refined and expanded. The longitudinal view indicated that the titles of each stage might be refined to accommodate a wider range of library users. The following discussion is limited to elaborations of the model based on the longitudinal study and is not a full description of the characteristics of each stage in the search process.

### Stage 1: Initiation

The essential element in the initiation stage is the presence of an information need. While a research assignment imposed an information need, the students internalized the task to create a personal need for meaning which motivated and directed their information-seeking activity. An assignment that invites a student to transform an imposed task into a need for meaning raises questions and problems which he or she can identify as worth pursuing. All of the participants in the study attempted to do this when given the opportunity.

**Stage 2: Selection**

The four criteria for selecting a topic in the original model were: personal interest, requirements of the assignment, information available, and time allotted. While the participants continued to use these criteria, this study noted that all were not of equal importance in every case. G described approaching topic selection in two ways in different assignments. In most instances, the information available took priority over personal interest, but in one assignment she described selecting a topic of personal interest although adequate information was not available. J repeatedly described giving priority to personal interest over the requirements of the assignment. For all 4 students, personal interest had become a more important criterion than it had been in high school as they moved toward an area of specialization and expertise.

**Stage 3: Exploration**

The subjects described the exploration stage as a search for information, from general to specific, but their explanations revealed a more heuristic process that could be quite disorderly and confusing at times rather than a neat step-by-step progression. For example, D and C described going back and forth from the card catalog to sources as they learned more about the topic, and "browsing" the shelves to seek out "buried" information.

The conceptual maps showed that as students matured they became more aware of the essential part that thinking plays throughout the search process. After entering college, their maps include active, cognitive concepts, such as think, worry, procrastinate, decide, discuss, read, reread, and organize. When students noted that they procrastinated at the beginning of a search, they applied a negative connotation to the preparatory thinking and mulling that characterizes this stage; such a trend also was evident in the high school case studies. Participants' descriptions of information seeking at this stage reveal the tendency to use sources they had on hand before reaching out for further information. First, they used sources already known or recommended and then they sought less accessible sources.

## Stage 4: Formulation

Formulation is the development of a focus which evolves from
thinking and reading about a problem or topic. The focus provides
direction for the collection of information. At this stage, decisions of
relevance change as a result of increased personal knowledge.

The students used metaphors to express their perceptions of
formulation. C described a thread to pull the separate parts together;
J used a story within the literature that made sense: D used the more
conventional theme of a focus, as did G in her reference to
narrowing the general topic. There was a combination of chance and
creativity in their descriptions of formulation. In several instances,
students used the term, "luck," which is more likely to be an "aha" of
recognition with increased personal knowledge and understanding.
G remembered finding one particular source that pulled things
together late in the process. She further noted that if she had come
to the source earlier, she might not have recognized its relevance.
These students described formulation taking place toward the middle
or latter part of the process after they had been searching for some
time.

The original model depicted stages three, four, and five as discrete
and separate. The present study revealed the stages from exploration
through collection as overlapping and merging. The participants
described a more heuristic, spiral process in which emerging thoughts
were changing and evolving, rather than a distinct formulation
point. Formulation, however, was seen as part of the search process
and was not postponed to the writing stage. While formulation
remained a difficult part of the search process, as college students,
they had become more articulate in describing their experience in
formulation than they had been in high school. Individual approaches to formulation seemed to remain consistent over time.

## Stage 5: Collection

When students explained their method of collecting information they
revealed a sense of ownership on an internal, intellectual, and private
level. There was an element of possession in the process as well as
product. Students had devised personal systems for collecting information which did not include all of the methods commonly taught in

traditional library instruction programs. Yellow pads replaced notecards for the most part. Outlining was used to organize for writing
and not earlier as is often recommended to organize for searching.
Systems of coding were devised and recall was considered as an
important component of organizing.

In addition to the due date of the paper, completion of a search was
determined by either the concept of exhausting sources or having
enough to present. Both perspectives were based on meeting the
original information need and the ability to present. The students had
personal standards that they consistently used to determine closure.

**Stage 6: Presentation**

Outlining was an important technique for organizing information
for presenting. G described her ease in writing a paper after she had
prepared a detailed outline for an oral presentation. The organization of information for giving to others was creatively approached
for the most part. However, D reported that she sometimes became
bored with her topic at this point and wanted to move on to
something new. There was evidence of personal ownership in the
topic and a frequent need to know more and to go further with the
research after an assignment was completed. As students matured,
their sense of ownership in their products increased. They were
actively seeking to build an area of expertise.

## MAJOR FINDINGS AND IMPLICATIONS FOR
## MEDIATION

These longitudinal studies further verified the model of the search
process developed in the initial study. As students used the library
throughout their college years, their perceptions of the search process
became more like the model. They came to expect their topic to change
and a central theme to evolve during a search for information. They
expected to become more interested as the search progresses. From
these studies, we cannot say what effect cognitive development, experience, or introduction to the model had on perceptions. The findings, however, provide a sound base for further research into the
nature of the experience of a search for information.

The five studies, including research questions, key findings and citations of the major papers, are summarized in Table 5-1.

Two areas of findings are worthy of particular attention because they have implications for library and information services. These are changes in perceptions of process and of interest, both of which may be general characteristics of more experienced users.

These longitudinal studies revealed changes in students' expectations of the search process as a sensemaking process occurring over time. They expected a topic to change and their thoughts to evolve during the process. They anticipated uncertainty as a normal beginning for their investigation and formulation. They had a sense of closure beyond that of running out of time.

In addition, of the four criteria for making decisions about topic and focus, personal interest received priority over assignment requirements, information available, and time allotted. They expected to become more interested in their topic as the search progressed.

Each of these areas of findings indicate direction for process intervention. One disheartening finding, however, was the perception of a minimal role for librarians and dissatisfaction expressed at the inadequate role that formal mediators played in their search process. While the students sought counseling and guidance in the evolving process from friends and family, librarians remained in the role of locator.

A longitudinal view of the information search process led to the following recommendations for intervening in the process of learning from information and of designing programs of instruction:

- An emphasis on the process of a search to promote an awareness of the sequence of feelings, thoughts, and actions commonly experienced in a search for information;
- The provision for situations that promote seeking a focus during a search for information; and
- An involvement in extended library searching that offers opportunities to experience increased interest as individuals learn more about a topic.

By viewing the findings of these studies in the frame of the constructionist theory of learning, we can propose a process theory for library and information services. The process theory is articu-

**Table 5-1.    Information Search Process (ISP): Questions
and Key Findings in Five Studies**

### Study 1 (1983)

*Research Question:* Do users' experiences in the ISP resemble the phases in the process of construction?

*Key Findings:* Common patterns in ISP correspond to process of construction in a 6-Stage Model.

*References:*

Kuhlthau, Carol C. (1985). "A Process Approach to Library Skills Instruction," *School Library Media Quarterly, 13*(1), 35–40.

_____ (1985). *Teaching the Library Research Process.* West Nyack, NY: The Center for Applied Research in Education.

_____ (1988). "Developing a Model of the Library Search Process: Cognitive and Affective Aspects," *Reference Quarterly, 28*(2), 232–242.

### Study 2 (1986)

*Research Question:* How had students' perceptions of the ISP changed after four years of college?

*Key Findings:* Perceptions of ISP became more like the model over time, particularly regarding focus and process.

*References:*

Kuhlthau, Carol C. (1988). "Perceptions of the Information Search Process in Libraries: A Study of Changes from High School Through College," *Information Processing and Management, 24*(4), 419–427.

### Study 3 (1987)

*Research Question:* What do longitudinal case studies reveal of students' internal view of the ISP after four years of undergraduate study?

*Key Findings:* ISP described as a purposeful, sensemaking process.

*References:*

Kuhlthau, Carol C. (1988). "Longitudinal Case Studies of the Information Search Process of Users in Libraries," *Library and Information Science Research, 10*(3), 257–304.

### Study 4 (1988)

*Research Question:* Do low- and middle-level high school seniors and other high achieving seniors experience the ISP as described in the model?

*Key Findings:* The model was confirmed in a larger, more diverse sample of high school seniors. In addition, there was an indication of a correlation between focus in research papers and change in confidence during search process.

*References:*

Kuhlthau, Carol C. (1989). "The Information Search Process of High-Middle-Low Achieving High School Seniors," *School Library Media Quarterly, 17*(4), 224–228.

_____ (1989). *The Information Search Process of High-Middle-Low Achieving High School Seniors.* Final Report of Study Funded by Rutgers Research Council, ERIC Clearinghouse on Information Resources, Syracuse University. (ED 310787).

*(continued on next page)*

**Table 5-1.** *(continued)*

**Study 5 (1989)**

*Research Question:* Does the model of the ISP hold for a large, diverse sample of library users?

*Key Findings:* The model was verified with academic, public, and school library users. While thoughts and feelings matched the model as anticipated, the identification of task did not.

*References:*

Kuhlthau, Carol C., Betty Turock, Mary W. George, and Robert J. Belvin (1990). Validating a Model of the Search Process: A Comparison of Academic, Public, and School Library Users. *Library and Information Science Research, 12*(1), 5–32.

Kuhlthau, Carol C., Betty J. Turock, Mary W. George and Robert J. Belvin. (1989). *Facilitating Information Seeking Through Cognitive Modeling of the Search Process.* Final Report. U.S. Department of Education, Library Research and Demonstration Grant G008720323–87, ERIC (ED 328268).

**Summary of the Findings:**

Kuhlthau, Carol C. (1989). "Information Search Process: A Summary of Research and Implications for School Library Media Programs," *School Library Media Quarterly, 18*(5), 19–25.

_____ (1991). "Inside the Search Process: Information Seeking from the User's Perspective." *Journal of the American Society for Information Science, 42*(5), 361–371.

lated as an uncertainty principle in the theoretical statement (see Chapter 7). Before discussing the theory, the methodology used for these series of studies warrants closer scrutiny and description. The next chapter provides that discussion.

Understanding perceptions opens the possibility of mediating directly into those areas that might be expected to cause difficulty in a search for information. Intervention can be tailored to the specific needs of an individual user or to those of a group of users. For example, people can be made more aware of the need to seek a focus for their search and be better prepared to meet the feelings of uncertainty that they might expect to experience as they progress toward a focus.

These studies indicate a deeper level of intervention in order to guide and counsel people in the process of learning from gaining access to information. Library and information services need to be redefined in terms of the user's experience in the process of seeking information.

# Chapter 6

## Methodology for Studying the Constructive Process of Information Seeking

When one views information seeking as a process of construction, the user's experience in that process becomes a critical component in information provision. Research into the experience of users requires methods which elicit the user's perspective rather than that of the librarian or the system. This is much easier said than done. Traditionally, user studies have placed the system squarely in the center of study as the unit of analysis. Many studies that claim the user to be the unit of analysis actually represent the position of the library or information system, and they merely seek the user's assessment of the system. In order to understand the user's experience, the system must be virtually ignored for a time, and attention must be placed solely on the process of the user.

Much of the traditional methodology employed in users studies is not appropriate for the investigation of users' experiences in the constructive process of information seeking. The shift of emphasis to users, and the cognitive aspects of information use, requires methods that reveal users' experiences. Internal processes are not readily observed in a study of behavior. Making inferences about the reasoning behind an act by merely observing the act is inadequate. Research methods need to open the user's experience for observation. There is need for innovative approaches and the development of new methods to reveal the information-seeking process from the user's perspective.

The methodology used in this research was founded on two assumptions: a longitudinal approach was necessary for studying a constructive process, and field studies rather than laboratory experiments were essential for eliciting real-life experience. The initial study comprised an exploratory base for an area of research rather than a complete entity in and of itself. In this sense, the overall research approach was longitudinal. There were five studies in the sequence, each one being a field study with a longitudinal approach. The subjects in each study were real people with real problems in real libraries.

A combination of qualitative and quantitative methods was applied to study many aspects of the problem over an extended period of time. The research process is related to the information search process in that problems evolve through different stages of formulation. Problems in early formative states may be best addressed by qualitative methods to form testable hypotheses, which can then be measured by more quantitative methods. The methods used in this research proceeded from qualitative to quantitative.

Qualitative and quantitative methods complimented each other by offering two ways of looking at the problem. Qualitative methods offered an internal view, which addressed the why of the issue, bringing insight to more quantitative findings. Qualitative methods offered ways to explore and investigate the obscure problem and to generate testable hypotheses. Methods involved small-scale studies using ethnographic-type data collection and analysis offering results on which to base grounded theory. Quantitative methods offered ways to verify findings and to test hypotheses. Methods involved large-scale studies using statistical analysis offering more generalizable results. Both methods, of course, needed to be pursued rigorously and with an empirical approach. Both also produced findings that led to the generation of further research questions.

In each phase of the research the problem being addressed determined the methodology adopted. The sequence of research questions required both qualitative and quantitative methods. The methods and instruments developed in the initial study were adapted and refined to address the questions of the subsequent studies in the series. The series of five studies on the information search process have emerged into an area of research, theory, and methodology that continues to open fruitful questions for further investigation, verification, and refinement.

## APPLICATION FOR METHODS IN LIBRARY AND INFORMATION SERVICES

The methodology described in this chapter was designed for empirical research and is intended to be applied and adapted in further research into information-seeking behavior. The development of this work offers an example of how theory may be built in a sequence of studies.

The methods may be utilized in developing a process approach to library and information services. There are two ways that these methods may be applied in library practice. One is as tools for action research. The methods and instruments described in this chapter provide ways of revealing the user's information search process and may be used in many different information settings for assessing and evaluating users' perspectives of services and their experience in the process of information seeking. In this way, these methods may be used as tools for assessing existing services and for identifying the need for a process approach as well as for measuring the effectiveness of process interventions.

Another use of the methods is as a means of developing self awareness in users. As these methods open the process for the observation of the researcher they also reveal the process to the user. The methods may be applied and adapted as interventions with users which enable them to understand the information search process as a process of learning from having access to information. At various points in this discussion of methodology, ways to use particular methods as process interventions will be noted.

## A QUALITATIVE BEGINNING

The initial study addressed the problem of understanding the user's experience in the process of seeking information? A number of research questions were addressed, but the primary ones were: Do users have common experiences in the process of information seeking that can be articulated and described? Do users' experiences resemble the phases in the process of construction?

The study was a qualitative exploration of students' experiences in completing assigned library research. Research methods were employed to seek the fullest description of the situation from the perspective of those directly involved; this foundation provided a base for grounded theory. Glaser and Strauss (1967) recommend the use of rigorous techniques to collect data that overlap and that offer multilayered descriptions providing an empirical basis for findings. In this way, an emerging theory was grounded in a real-life situation.

The study was conducted in a large, eastern, suburban high school with a group of academically capable high school seniors (Kuhlthau, 1983). Academic capability was determined by standardized test scores above 90 percent using national percentiles and grade point averages. The students selected were expected to be the most proficient in the high school population at using the library for completing research assignments. The objectives were to investigate the search process of *successful* students and to observe the strategies they used to work through the process. Subjects were chosen based on their ability and willingness to recall and discuss the library search process as they experienced it.

The students were studied in the natural setting of their school library media center. Two research papers were assigned in their English course, one each semester of the school year, in which they were given considerable latitude in selecting topics.

Instruments and methods were designed to reveal aspects of the search process that would otherwise be hidden from an observer. Developing methods for observing the search process was an important aspect of the initial study. Each method and instrument was assessed for its effectiveness in eliciting the user's perspective of the process of information seeking. The qualitative methods used were journals, search logs, short written statements, case study interviews and conceptual maps, and the teacher's assessment of focus in the students' papers. A questionnaire to elicit perceptions was the beginning of the development of more quantitative instruments.

## Journals

The students kept journals during their completion of the first assignment in which they were asked to record their feelings as well as the thoughts and actions related to their library search. They were directed to record thoughts and conversations they had about their topics outside of the library, as well as within it. Students submitted the journals, together with their papers, at the end of the assignment.

Journals gave students an opportunity to include personal content and what they considered to be important about their search without placing restrictions on the format or length of the entries. While some students made fuller, more consistent entries than others, all recorded the progression of their thoughts and feelings. The students displayed highly individual styles in keeping their journals — some consistently made descriptive entries, while others summarily recorded their actions or made only an occasional, incomplete entry. Many students made several entries at once rather than recording their search separately on each day. All journals reflected changes in student understanding of the topic from the time that they first selected that topic.

**Search Logs**

While working on the second assignment, students kept search logs in which they recorded the names of the sources they used, procedures for finding sources, and whether sources were useful, highly useful, or not useful (see Figure 6–1).

Search logs were effective for tracking the sources used and for making relevance judgments as the search progressed. Unlike the unstructured writing of the journal, the search log did not offer an opportunity to include feelings. It did, however, provide data on the decisions made about the relevance of the sources consulted during a search, and the log offered another way of examining the progression of thoughts and actions. Further study is needed to develop and analyze the search log method. An interesting outcome was that some of the sources considered not useful early in the search were included in the bibliography of the papers. This may indicate a change in decision of relevancy as a search progresses, or it may simply be a result of padding the bibliography. Based on these findings, further research into decisions of relevance and pertinence at various points in a search is warranted. The responses on the search logs were charted to track patterns of choices made during the progress of the search. Patterns of "somewhat useful," "most useful," and "not useful" were expected to be evident. While the

**Topic: Transcendentalism & Emerson**

| DATE | TITLE | CALL NO. | LOCATED IN | NOT USEFUL | SOMEWHAT USEFUL | MOST USEFUL |
|---|---|---|---|---|---|---|
| 3/3/82 | B EME Ralph Waldo Emerson Portrait of a Balanced Soul AUTHOR Edward Wagenknecht PUBLISHER DATE Oxford University Press NY 1974 | | Public Library | | X | |
| 3/5/82 | American Transcendentalism: An Anthology of Criticism Brian M. Barbour, ed. University of Notre Dame Press 1973 141 BAR | | Media Center | | | X |

**FIG. 6–1.  Search Log**

results were inconclusive the method shows promise for further development.

## Short Written Statements

Participants were asked to write a paragraph about their topic two weeks after the assignment was made and again after they had submitted their papers. It was assumed that the ability or inability to express a central idea in writing would indicate the state of their thinking about the topic. The method was analyzed for effectiveness in revealing the formulation of a focus.

Writing a paragraph about the topic at the middle and again at the end of the search proved effective in revealing the students' thoughts at a particular point. All of the students wrote a paragraph about their topic or focus in the two writing sessions. A change in all of their writings was apparent between the first and second writing. However, some had difficulty expressing a central theme or focus for their topic in the written statements.

## Case Studies

While there is not a proliferation of case studies in library and information science research, there are substantial precedents for the use of the method. Some examples of case study research are Ford's (1986) study of psychological determinants of information needs of higher education students and Blackie and Smith's (1981) study of situational influences and constraints on undergraduate information seekers. Prentice (1980) presents case studies to describe information seeking of persons from various backgrounds. She summaries differences and similarities in an approach not unlike the one reported in this work.

Case studies offered an important, if not essential, way of collecting data on users' experiences, perceptions, and choices affecting the information search process. Interviews allowed subjects to explain their actions and to elaborate on perceptions that lie behind action. The students had an opportunity to tell how the search process works as they see it. Case studies provided a potential method for checking on the researcher's assumptions and findings in the realm of personal experience.

Six students volunteered to be case study subjects in order to clarify and explain the data collected in the journals, logs, writings, and questionnaires of the total sample. Case studies provided indepth insights into not only what was happening but also why it was. These subjects were interviewed in 45-minute taped sessions on 6 separate occasions during completion of the two research assignments. The interviews were designed to examine the particular stage of the process that participants experienced at the time. The following are examples of the points and questions to which the students responded:

- Describe how you felt when the teacher announced the research assignment.
- Describe how and why you chose your topic.
- Describe any focus your topic has taken.
- Describe any choices you have made in your search that gave you just the information you were looking for, changed your mind about your topic, led you to new understanding, or gave you direction.

- How did you know when your search was completed?
- Describe the conclusion of your search and how you feel about your work.
- What did you find most difficult about your search?

Interviews were an exceedingly effective method for investigating the students' interpretations and explanations of what had occurred during the search process. Student were asked similar questions but they were urged to elaborate on personal experiences. They were cooperative and willing to participate in these discussions during the six interviews. Their responses were analyzed for both individual approaches and common experiences.

**Conceptual Maps**

Two other methods, flowcharts and timelines as conceptual maps of the search process, were used to collect data on the six interview subjects. Concept mapping is the general term for the method of graphically depicting mental relationships, logic, or strategies. Flow-charting, widely used in systems analysis and programming, can be adapted as one technique for capturing a person's concept or mental map. In research on information use, flowcharting has been applied most frequently as a method of data analysis. Dervin, Jacobsen, and Nilan (1982) used timelines as a research technique, and Taylor (1968), among others, employed flowcharting. In this study, however, flowcharts and timelines were used as methods of data collection since users diagrammed their own perceptions of the information search process.

At the end of the first assignment, the six were asked to describe the progression of their search by drawing a timeline including all important decisions. They drew timelines, after having completed a research project, by referring to their journals to document particular dates and events. They were given a paper on which a horizontal line was drawn and told that the beginning of the line represented when they had received the assignment and the end when they began to write their paper. They were asked to fill in a timeline of what had taken place in the search that they had just completed.

At the end of the second assignment, they were asked to draw flowcharts of the process they had followed. The subjects were given instructions similar to those for the timeline. In this instance, however, the upper-left corner represented when they had received the assignment and the lower-right corner when they began to write their paper.

Timelines and flowcharts were ways of mapping and diagramming the progression of a search. All 6 interviewees identified a sequence of steps and strategies on the timelines and flowcharts. The timelines were analyzed for revealing stages in the search process and the evolution of the topic. The flowcharts were analyzed for patterns of prediction and choice in the search and evidence of a process taking place.

## Teachers' Assessment

At the end of each assignment, in addition to assigning a grade, the teacher characterized each student paper as having a vague, general, or clear focus. It was assumed that those students who understood the process in which they were involved and knew strategies for using the library to work through the search process would have clearly focused papers.

## Perceptions Questionnaire

The Perceptions Questionnaire was an early attempt at developing a quantitative instrument to elicit users' perceptions of information seeking in libraries. Perceptions are difficult to observe and are not normally seen by merely watching individuals while they use a library. The development of a questionnaire to elicit perceptions of users was an important aspect of the study. Rather than testing knowledge of sources, a method was sought to identify perceptions of the process of a search that would influence the way that students approach a search. A questionnaire was designed to examine students' perceptions of six areas of library use: general library use, topic selection, research assignments, focus formulation, procedures for gathering information, and role of mediators. Thirty statements were developed on the areas of library use under investigation and were intermixed on a questionnaire, using a 5-point Likert scale, with 5 being "almost always" and 1 becoming "almost never" (see Table 6-1).

## Table 6-1.   Perceptions Questionnaire I

| | Almost Always | Often | Sometimes | Seldom | Almost Never |
|---|---|---|---|---|---|
| 1. I use more than one library to research a topic. | | | | | |
| 2. I prefer research topics suggested by the teacher. | | | | | |
| 3. I use the library to gather information on my own, not connected to an assignment by a teacher. | | | | | |
| 4. I use more than two libraries to research a topic. | | | | | |
| 5. I prefer research topics that I choose myself. | | | | | |
| 6. I get help from a teacher when choosing a research topic. | | | | | |
| 7. When researching a topic I need the librarians' assistance. | | | | | |
| 8. I talk to others about possible topics before making a final choice of a research topic. | | | | | |
| 9. The card catalog is the first place I check when researching a topic. | | | | | |
| 10. I try to select a topic that relates to another paper I have written. | | | | | |
| 11. My teacher helps me to gather information. | | | | | |
| 12. I talk to others about my topic. | | | | | |
| 13. I use reference books when gathering information about a topic. | | | | | |
| 14. I select a topic that I know little about. | | | | | |
| 15. I have difficulty finding information on a topic. | | | | | |

**Table 6–1.** *(continued)*

| | Almost Always | Often | Sometimes | Seldom | Almost Never |
|---|---|---|---|---|---|

16. I spend free time in the library.
17. I become more interested in a topic as I gather information.
18. I use periodicals when researching a topic.
19. I have difficulty selecting a topic for a research paper.
20. A central theme evolves as I gather information on a topic.
21. I use indexes in the back of books to find information on a topic.
22. When I first choose a topic I have a clear idea about what I will find and write about.
23. Research assignments add to what I learn in a course.
24. Researching a topic takes more time than I anticipate.
25. When selecting and developing a research topic I use information from television.
26. My topic changes as I gather information about it.
27. I change my topic according to the materials that are available.
28. I ask a librarian for help before I have chosen my topic.
29. I use the library when I want to select books to read.
30. I ask a librarian for assistance after I have chosen a research topic.

The questionnaire was analyzed for ease of administering, students' willingness to participate, time for administering, and effectiveness for revealing perceptions of the group and as well as those of individuals.

The questionnaire took approximately 12 minutes to administer, with students completing their responses in 6 to 10 minutes and the instructions given in approximately 2 minutes. The questions were easily understood and able to be answered without undue deliberation. The scale was appropriate for the content and type of questions that the students were asked. The questionnaire was suitable for surveying a group of students. The responses indicated students' impressions that provided the basis for making inferences about the perceptions they held.

## APPLICATION OF METHODS FOR PROCESS INTERVENTION

All these methods may be adopted as process interventions. Journal keeping has been particularly helpful for people involved in an extensive information-seeking project. In the early stages of the search process, journal writing provides a vehicle for formulating thoughts and for identifying unclear areas needing investigation. In the later stages, the journal may be used as a notebook for developing a position with supporting information. Search logs are more of a bibliographic tool and may be used in place of notecards to develop the concept of an emerging process. The main purpose of the log is to keep track of all references and to note which ones may be of particular use at a specific point in the search process. These judgments of usefulness may change as the search progresses.

Written statements help people to identify where they are in the search process. Those unable to write a paragraph on the main points in their work probably have not reached a focused perspective and are in the exploration stage. Such statements need not always be written but may occur in conversation with the mediator. Brief statements about the status of the user's thinking enable the mediator to diagnose the state of the problem and to determine what strategies would be most appropriate and helpful at a particular point in the process.

Conceptual maps in the form of timelines and flowcharts briefly summarize an individual's search process. These maps and charts are extremely useful for assessing a search after its conclusion in order to identify problems that might be avoided next time, as well as to point out useful strategies to be repeated in other information need situations.

The questionnaire to elicit perceptions related to libraries and information seeking that was designed for high school students has been adapted for use outside of this population. A questionnaire based on a Likert scale is a good action research tool for assessing perceptions before and after conducting interventions. The questionnaire may serve as an example for developing an instrument for a specific setting and a particular group.

## ANALYSIS OF QUALITATIVE DATA

The objective of analyzing the collected data was to test the constructivist approach to learning within the information-seeking activity of students in the process of doing library research. Evidence was sought to support the theoretical assumption that students' experiences in the search process would match those in the phases of construction and document similar accompanying feelings.

The students' experience in the assigned library research was analyzed to develop a model of the stages of the search process that they completed; these stages included feelings, thoughts, and actions. Content analysis was used with categories derived from the theory base, particularly Kelly's Phases of Construction. The search was thought of as a process with a beginning, a middle, and an end. The students' descriptions of the beginning of a search were grouped together, as were their descriptions of the middle and the end of a search. The data collected were analyzed to discover patterns of common experience at particular points in a search.

A description of the search process was sought through the data collected from the application of the methods designed in the study. The students' journals, search logs, writings as well as the case study subjects' interviews, timelines, and flowcharts were examined for evidence of stages in the search process and the characteristics that might be common to each stage. Six categories of characteristics were sought for each stage: task, thoughts, feelings, actions, strategies, and mood.

The task of each stage in the search process was analyzed as the students commonly interpreted the task. The tasks were identified within the process of accomplishing the ultimate goal of writing a research paper.

The thoughts and feelings that accompany the action of the search for information were examined. While source or system orientation of library use would concentrate on the actions of a library search, process or user orientation need to consider the thoughts and feelings that prompt actions. Thoughts and feelings that were commonly experienced were sought within the stages of the search process.

Students' expression of their thoughts was examined to determine their state of understanding of the topic under investigation and to discover evidence of developing clarity and focus. The feelings that accompany the search process were analyzed within the frame of reference of Kelly's phases of construction: confusion, doubt, threat, hypothesis formulation, testing, reassessing, and reconstruing. The actions of each stage were examined for the underlying predictions and choices made by students that determined the direction of their actions. Students' choices were analyzed within Kelly's categories of choices for extension and for definition to determine if either type were characteristic of specific stages in the process. Evidence of choices that were particularly significant or had an "elaborative effect" on the search was sought.

The function of a focus as an elaborative choice in the process was an important consideration in the study. The focus in the search process was expected to parallel the role of the hypothesis in the phases of construction. As the hypothesis was crucial to the phases of construction, the user's perception that a focus must be formed within the search process was considered as a critical element for moving the search to completion. The descriptions of the middle of the search were analyzed for evidence of a turning point, as were the teacher's assessment of a focus in the students' papers.

Evidence of the presence of an invitational mood or an indicative mood was sought as indication of how attitude and stance might effect the search process. Characteristics of the search process were sought to develop a model of the process that would demonstrate the common experience of users.

## HYPOTHESIS FOR FURTHER STUDY: A MODEL

Testable hypotheses were generated in this qualitative study in the form of a model of the information search process in six stages. Chapter 4 describes the findings of the initial study and the model developed from the findings. In addition, Chapter 5 discusses the findings of the subsequent four studies in the sequence which verified and refined the model (see Table 5-1).

Two approaches were taken to verify the findings of the exploratory study. One was a large-scale approach using a more diversified sample and the other was a longitudinal approach using the original sample. In the large-scale approach a diverse sample of high school students was studied as well as library users in academic and public libraries. In the longitudinal approach, the same panel of library users in the initial study were studied 4 years later. By combining the two verification approaches, using both quantitative and qualitative methods, general and indepth results were obtained.

## LARGE-SCALE VERIFICATION

The verification studies were designed to collect data on the thoughts, feelings, and actions of library users in the process of an extended search for information. Although the data had certain qualitative characteristics, quantitative analysis was required for verification. Two methods were applied for preparing the data for analysis. One was that nominal-level data were treated as ordinal, assumed-level data in order to perform statistical measures. The other was that open-ended responses were coded into categorical data for statistical analysis.

### Diverse Sample of High School Seniors

*Research Question:* Do low- and middle-level high school seniors and other high-achieving seniors experience the Information Search process as described in the Model?

Six high schools in New Jersey representing a diverse population were selected as sites for the study. Low-, Middle-, and High-achieving seniors in homogeneously grouped English classes were selected on the basis of their grade-point averages and national percentile scores on a standardized test. There were 147 participants: 34 in the group were identified as high achievers, 73 middle college-bound, and 40 of the lower-level achievers.

Each participant was assigned an English paper requiring library research on a topic of the student's choice related to the course. The paper was limited to 5 pages, but the number and variety of sources were not specified. The project was to be completed in 4 weeks, during which time the librarians taught 5 predesigned instructional sessions on the search process taken from *Teaching the Library Research Process* (Kuhlthau, 1985b).

**Process Surveys**

The process surveys were designed to elicit cognitive and affective aspects of the information search process as the journal, search log, and written statements had in the initial study. The instrument was intended to collect data from a large sample which could be analyzed and compared. The objective was to elicit experience in terms of thoughts, feelings, and actions at the beginning, middle, and end of the search process.

The surveys were made up of 6 questions, the first 4 related to thoughts (name the source you are using; what you are looking for; state the title of your project; what your topic is about) and the last 2 related to feelings (rate your confidence level using a scale of 1 as low to 10 as high, and write three adjectives describing how you feel). The librarians at each site administered a process survey at three points, at the beginning (Initiation), in the middle (Midpoint), and toward the end (Closure).

Responses to the questions related to thoughts were coded by two coders as follows: 1 for general or background thoughts, 2 for more specific ideas or narrowing of the general topic, and 3 for a focused perspective of a personal point of view. A Thoughts Index was derived from a simple additive of nominal data treated as an assumed interval scale with aggregate scores which ranged from 4 minimum to 12 maximum. The aggregate scores were then tested for significant change at the three points in the search process.

From the responses to the questions related to feelings, an interval

Confidence Scale, ranging from 1 as low to 10 as high, was devised. The confidence level was compared at the three points in the search process to determine significant changes as were the adjectives listed by participants to describe their feelings.

In addition, the teachers assessed each student paper for evidence of focus on a scale of 1 as low to 10 as high, and listed the number and variety of sources cited in the bibliography. The grades given to the papers by the teachers were also collected. Changes in confidence level as found in the process surveys were then compared to the teachers' assessments to determine if there were correlations.

Statistical analysis was made by using t-tests and analysis of variance (ANOVA) to determine significance, and Pearson product-moment measures to determine degree of correlation and measures of linear regression.

## Sample of Academic, Public, and School Library Users

*Research Question:* Does the Model of the Information Search Process hold for a large, diverse sample of library users?

Further testing of the model of the Information Search Process was conducted in a large-scale study with 385 academic, public, and school library users in 21 sites (Kuhlthau, Turock, George, and Belvin, 1990). The study was conducted in field situations with actual library users, most of whom were responding to an imposed rather than a personally initiated or job-related problem.

Field sites were chosen on the basis of their location, size, receptivity to innovation, and willingness to participate in all phases of the study. In the final sample there were 8 school, 7 academic, and 6 public library sites. The librarians at each location selected up to 30 library users on the basis of the suitability of their information problem and their willingness to participate in the study. Only research-level questions that would be completed within the 12-week period of the study were considered.

The academic library sample was composed of undergraduate students; neither faculty nor graduate students were included. The public library sample was limited to mature adults; high school and college students were not included. The school library sample was composed of 10th- to 12th-grade students. Of the 385 library users who participated in the study, 59 percent (229) were from school library media centers, 28 percent (108) were from academic libraries, and 13 percent (48) were from public libraries.

Three instruments were used to collect data, a Process Survey, a Conceptual Map, and a Perceptions Questionnaire, each of which were adapted from those designed in the prior studies.

## Process Survey

The Process Survey was adapted to elicit experiences in the Information Search Process as described in the model of a large, diverse sample of library users as shown in Table 6-2. Changes were made to facilitate comparative analysis and to test the model with more detail and precision. A 9-question survey was developed with the first 4 questions eliciting openended responses and the others selections from a list of choices taken directly from the model. The surveys were administered to each of the participants at three points— initiation, midpoint, and closure—in their search.

The first step of the data analysis involved producing descriptive statistics, including frequency distributions and measures of central tendency. In preparation for this step, responses on the Process Survey were coded. The first 4 questions: "What are you looking for?," "Describe your topic in a short paragraph," "What is the title of your project?," and "Who have you talked to about your project?" elicited open-ended responses, resulting in categorical data as shown in Table 6-3. Question 5 asked the respondents to identify their confidence level on a 10-point scale at three different stages of the project: Initiation, Midpoint, and Closure. This question was analyzed as if the data were interval.

An attempt was made to elicit the respondents' feelings with Question 6, "From the adjectives below, check those that describe how you feel at this point in the project." Multiple responses were expected because no limit was put upon the number which could be selected. In order to show both response and nonresponse, each item within these questions was entered as a separate variable, coded "1" to show that the item had been selected, or "0" to show that it had not been selected. This yielded sets of dichotomous variables, which were treated as interval-level data. Question 7, "What is your task now?" limited responses to only one choice, each of which was then

## Table 6-2. Process Survey

Date _____          Number _____

### INITIATION

1. What are you looking for?
2. Describe the topic in a short paragraph.
3. What is the title of your project?
4. Who have you talked to about your project?
5. On the scale below indicate your confidence level at this point in the project.

```
 ├──┼──┼──┼──┼──┼──┼──┼──┼──┤
 1    2    3    4    5    6    7    8    9    10
 Low                                    High
```

6. From the adjectives below, check those that describe how you feel at this point in the project.

   ☐ Confident          ☐ Confused
   ☐ Disappointed       ☐ Doubtful
   ☐ Frustrated         ☐ Optimistic
   ☐ Relieved           ☐ Satisfied
   ☐ Sure               ☐ Uncertain
   ☐ Other _____

7. What is your task now? Please check one box.

   ☐ To gather information pertaining to the specific topic.
   ☐ To investigate information on the general topic.
   ☐ To complete the information search.
   ☐ To recognize an information need.
   ☐ To formulate a specific topic.
   ☐ To identify the general topic.
   ☐ Other _____

8. What are you doing now? Check as many boxes as apply to you.

   ☐ Discussing the topic.
   ☐ Making a comprehensive search of the library.
   ☐ Browsing in the library.
   ☐ Outlining to organize information.
   ☐ Reading over notes for themes.
   ☐ Making a preliminary search of the library.
   ☐ Conferring with people who know about the topic.
   ☐ Asking librarian questions.
   ☐ Talking about themes and ideas.
   ☐ Making a summary search of the library.
   ☐ Skimming and scanning sources of information.
   ☐ Writing about themes and ideas.
   ☐ Reading about topic.
   ☐ Taking detailed notes on facts and ideas.
   ☐ Taking brief notes of facts and ideas.
   ☐ Rechecking sources for information initially overlooked.
   ☐ Recording bibliographic citations.
   ☐ Other _____

*(continued on next page)*

---

**Table 6–2.** *(continued)*

---

9. What are you thinking now? Check as many boxes as apply to you.
   ☐ Organizing ideas and information.
   ☐ Identifying possible alternative topics.
   ☐ Becoming informed about the general topic.
   ☐ Exhausting all possible sources of information.
   ☐ Considering alternative topics in light of the information available to me.
   ☐ Choosing the broad topic that has the potential for success.
   ☐ Comprehending the task before me.
   ☐ Recognizing ways to draw project to close.
   ☐ Considering alternative topics in light of the time I have to complete the project.
   ☐ Choosing specific concentrations within the general topic.
   ☐ Considering alternative topics in light of the requirements of the project.
   ☐ Confronting the inconsistency and incompatibility in the information encountered.
   ☐ Getting more interested and involved in ideas.
   ☐ Defining and extending my specific topic.
   ☐ Gaining a sense of direction and clarity.
   ☐ Recalling a previous project when I searched for information.
   ☐ Predicting success of each possible concentration.
   ☐ Identifying several possible areas of concentration in the broad topic.
   ☐ Considering alternative topics in light of the things that are of personal interest to me.
   ☐ Seeking information about my specific area of concentration.
   ☐ Other _____

---

coded from 1 to 7, resulting in categorical data. Question 8, "What are you doing now?," and Question 9, "What are you thinking now?," elicited multiple responses, which were coded in the same manner as Question 6. Frequencies and percentages were calculated from the data.

The second step of data analysis involved producing inferential statistics, including measures of significant difference and analysis of variance. Analysis of the Process Survey's Questions 1–4 was limited to the construction of contingency tables and single sample chi-square tests. Question 5, the confidence scale, was analyzed using paired t-tests between the Initiation, Midpoint, and Closure responses. The t-tests were performed on aggregated data by site and as repeated measures on each variable from Questions 5, 6, 8, and 9.

In each instance where a t-test was performed, the more conservative separate estimate of variance and, whenever possible, the

**Table 6–3.   Process Survey Coding**

Q1. What are you looking for?
    1 = General Information (Background)
    2 = Specific Information (Relevant)
    3 = Pertinent Information (Focused)
Q2. Describe topic in a short paragraph.
    1 = General Topic
    2 = Narrowed Topic
    3 = Focused point of view
Q3. What is the title of your project?
    1 = Vague concise expression
    2 = Clearer concise expression
    3 = Compromised concise expression
Q4. Who have you talked to about your project?
    1 = Other (Friend, family member)
    2 = Peer (Person also doing project)
    3 = Expert (Person who knows about topic)
    4 = Professional (Person who knows about sources)

paired t-test were used. A two-tailed probability of significance was applied. ANOVA was performed on variables aggregated by site, and the Scheffê test was used to indicate significant differences between group means. The nominal-level data of items selected in Questions 6, 8, and 9 were treated as assumed-interval data. However, in keeping with the actual measures involved, chi-square tests were also performed whenever any analysis of difference by group was done using interval tests, such as t-tests and ANOVA.

## Conceptual Maps

Participants were also asked to depict their views of the search process in two flowcharts, one at the beginning of their extended information-seeking projects and the other as they completed their searches. Only two limitations were placed on the diagrams: space was limited to one side of a standard page, and participants were told to draw and connect boxes; no further flowcharting instructions were given. By providing only a point of entry, "Initiate project," and a point of exit, "Information Search Completed," the instrument allowed participants freedom to depict their own mental maps of the search process. Note that this activity sought to elicit users' perceptions of the Information Search Process and not actual accounts of a search in progress.

This unstructured flowcharting resulted in a diversity of data that proved difficult for comparative analysis. The results were meaningful, however, in the context of the larger study and within the frame of reference of the model of the Information Search Process under investigation (Kuhlthau, Belvin, and George, 1989).

**Perceptions Questionnaire**

Users' perceptions of the search process and the role of mediators were tested by a Perceptions Questionnaire, administered before and after the search, as shown in Table 6–4. Statements on the Perceptions Questionnaire were based upon characteristics of process orientation as defined in the earlier study. Of the 20 questions, 10 were related to process and 10 to the role of mediators. A 4-point Likert scale of "almost always," "often," "seldom," and "almost never," was supplied for respondents.

Items on the Likert-scaled Perceptions Questionnaire ranged from a minimum value of 1 (almost always) to a maximum of 4 (almost never), with a mean of 2.5 for each item. Five questions on the Perceptions Questionnaire were written to elicit an ideal response of "almost never" rather than "almost always" and were reversed for coding and analysis. The responses to the Perceptions Questionnaire were collapsed into a dichotomous nominal variable as either matching the anticipated response or contradicting the anticipated response. Additional analysis was performed on these responses as ordinal, assumed-interval data. The t-tests were used both on the aggregated data by site and as repeated measures.

## APPLICATION OF METHODS FOR PROCESS INTERVENTIONS

The questionnaire and surveys described in this section were developed for assessing the search process in a quantitative way and may be applied across types of libraries with many different users. The questionnaire may be used for eliciting and comparing perceptions related to information seeking before and after interventions. They

## Table 6-4. Perception Questionnaire II

### THE INFORMATION SEARCH PROCESS

Date _____     Code _____

|  |  | Almost Always | Often | Seldom | Almost Never |
|---|---|---|---|---|---|
| 1. | I have a clear focus for my topic before using the library. | ☐ | ☐ | ☐ | ☐ |
| 2. | I find it helpful to talk to others about my topic. | ☐ | ☐ | ☐ | ☐ |
| 3. | My thoughts about my topic change as I explore information. | ☐ | ☐ | ☐ | ☐ |
| 4. | I like to find everything I will need first and then read it. | ☐ | ☐ | ☐ | ☐ |
| 5. | The library has the information I need. | ☐ | ☐ | ☐ | ☐ |
| 6. | A focus emerges as I gather information on a topic. | ☐ | ☐ | ☐ | ☐ |
| 7. | The information that I find at the beginning of a search is confusing and doesn't fit in with what I know. | ☐ | ☐ | ☐ | ☐ |
| 8. | I take detailed notes from every source of information I look at. | ☐ | ☐ | ☐ | ☐ |
| 9. | I ask the librarian for direction in locating materials in the library. | ☐ | ☐ | ☐ | ☐ |
| 10. | A search is completed when I no longer find new information. | ☐ | ☐ | ☐ | ☐ |
| 11. | All the sources of information I need are listed in the card catalog. | ☐ | ☐ | ☐ | ☐ |
| 12. | A search is completed when I find enough information. | ☐ | ☐ | ☐ | ☐ |
| 13. | I talk to people who know about my topic. | ☐ | ☐ | ☐ | ☐ |
| 14. | I become more interested in a topic as I gather information. | ☐ | ☐ | ☐ | ☐ |
| 15. | The information I need is in unexpected places in the library. | ☐ | ☐ | ☐ | ☐ |
| 16. | I make several trips to the library to research a topic. | ☐ | ☐ | ☐ | ☐ |
| 17. | I am successful in using the library. | ☐ | ☐ | ☐ | ☐ |
| 18. | I ask the librarian for advice on exploring a topic. | ☐ | ☐ | ☐ | ☐ |
| 19. | I ask the librarian for assistance in identifying materials. | ☐ | ☐ | ☐ | ☐ |
| 20. | I need materials other than books. | ☐ | ☐ | ☐ | ☐ |

may be used intact as presented in the Tables 6–2 and 6–4, or they
may be adapted for use in a specific situation.

The survey is an instrument for tracking progress during the
process of a search by making comparisons of responses at Initiation, Midpoint, and Closure. This instrument may be used as a tool
for action research using the coding system supplied in Table 6–3. It
may also be applied in a less formal way as a process intervention.
Users may track their own searches by responding to the survey at
three points in their process and by comparing their responses when
they have concluded the search. Applied in this way, the survey is an
instrument for heightening the user's awareness of her or his own
process.

## LONGITUDINAL VERIFICATION

Two longitudinal studies were conducted, one used quantitative
methods for gathering data and statistical methods for analyzing
data, and the other applied the qualitative approach of case study.
The first section describes the methods used in the quantitative
study.

### A Quantitative Approach

*Research Question:* How had students' perceptions of the Information Search Process changed after four years of college?

A longitudinal study was conducted to verify further the model by
addressing the question of whether individuals with extensive experience in using libraries and an introduction to the model have
perceptions that more closely match the model of the search process.
The research hypotheses in this study are as follows:

- Perceptions of library use change with exposure to the model
  of the search process;
- Perceptions of library use change with library experience; and
- The perception that a search is a process of evolving and
  changing thoughts contributes to the success of the outcome
  of a search.

This study assessed students at the beginning of their senior year in high school and after four years of college. The participants were the same students who had been selected for study when they were high school seniors during the 1981-1982 school year. All of the group subsequently attended four-year colleges and had completed college by June 1986 with the exception of two students who were intending to complete their requirements during the next academic year. The perceptions that these students had of the library research process were likely to indicate some expectations that promote productive library use. Changes during college would indicate ways that they had refined their perceptions in response to their actual experience in the process of searching for information. This study examined perceptions and did not track students in the progress of a search.

**Perceptions Questionnaire**

The study was based on responses to the questionnaire given to the students at the beginning of their senior year in high school and again to the same group of students, more than four years later — at the end of their senior year in college. Some 20 students responded to the follow-up study. The longitudinal element in the study provided a means of comparison and analysis of change in perceptions.

In high school, the questionnaire was administered directly in a class setting with the librarian giving instructions. The model of the search process was presented to them sometime later during their senior year. In college, the students were mailed the questionnaire with instructions for completion and return. They were asked three additional questions related to their library use when they were undergraduates: the number of papers they were assigned, how well prepared they were to research the papers, and what more they needed from their high school experience. They were also invited to make any further comments in writing.

An analysis of the responses was made within the six areas of library use elicited by the questionnaire. The participants' responses when they were undergraduates were compared with those they had made in high school to identify any changes in perceptions. With the expectation that the students' perceptions would change in the direction of the model of the search process, one-tailed t-tests were used to determine if there were significant differences between the

students' responses in high school and college. The comments written
by the students when they were in college were examined for the
extent of their library experience and how they might have been
better prepared for college library use.

## A Qualitative Approach

*Research Question:* What do longitudinal case studies reveal of
students' internal views of the Information Search Process after four
years of undergraduate study?

The present study provides a longitudinal perspective on four case
studies which were part of the earlier study. A panel of 4 students
who were the subjects of case studies when they were seniors in high
school were studied again after they had completed four years of
undergraduate education with the prospect of continuing the investigation through their experience in graduate study or situations of
employment in future studies. The indepth individual case study was
extended over a period of four years to examine patterns and changes
in personal perspectives. Where the original case study offered
insight into the perceptions of the subjects over an extended search
process, this study revealed their perceptions of information use at
two different points in their lives as students. Changes were traced as
well as was consistency in styles and preferences.

The study was based on subjects' recall and introspection, and not
on direct interaction with a librarian or information system. The
study was composed of the participants' explanations of the search
process and the information system. Further, the study examined the
user's perception of information seeking and information systems.

The researcher sought to remain interested but neutral during the
interviews. The user's perspective was elicited without value judgments or correction imposed by the researcher. The participants'
recollections and reactions were accepted as true. The emphasis of
this inquiry was on the nature of the process of seeking information,
not on the location and use of specific sources. The users' recollected
thoughts, actions and feelings were the central foci of the study.

The subjects of the original case studies were contacted after
completing four years of undergraduate study, with 4 of the 6 able to
participate in interviews and cognitive mapping exercises. All 4

participants had achieved academic success in college and were planning to enter graduate programs. Two of the students were male and two female.

**Case Studies: Interviews and Conceptual Maps**

Interviews and conceptual mapping provide an understanding of an individual's personal experience in the search process. The decision was made to continue tracking the case study subjects via two methods used in the initial study, interview and conceptual mapping, and to trace consistencies and changes in their perceptions of their experience after four years of college.

A 1-hour interview was conducted individually with each subject. Each interview was recorded and subsequently transcribed. The interview consisted of the following 10 questions and points:

- How often have you been given a research assignment in college?
- Describe some of the topics of past research assignments.
- How do you feel when a research assignment is announced?
- Describe the way you chose some of the topics for your research papers.
- Describe the procedure you follow when researching for a paper.
- Describe how you use the library at the beginning of research, at the middle, and at the end (before writing the paper).
- How did librarians assist you (instruction, reference)? How could librarians be more helpful?
- What is the most difficult part of a research assignment? Why?
- How could you have been better prepared for college research?
- How do you know when a search is completed?

In addition each participant was asked to draw on a timeline the process of a search as they commonly experienced it. The timelines provided a conceptual map of the subjects' perceptions of the search process based on their recall of, and reflection on, their search experience.

They were not shown the earlier renditions prior to drawing the timelines after college. The college timelines chart a generic rather than a specific search. Although the timelines drawn in high school do not precisely parallel those drawn after college, they were used to reveal patterns and to make a rough diagnoses. Future studies need to refine the mapping methodology.

The interviews of each case study participant were analyzed under the following five categories; selection of topic, attitude toward research assignments, perceptions of searching, procedures for gathering and organizing information, and the role of mediators. Comparisons were made with each participant's high school case study. Each student's conceptual map was compared with the one that he or she had drawn during high school. Consistent patterns as well as evidence of change were sought in each participant's description of the search process.

The interviews and conceptual maps of the 4 participants were then compared with each other under the same five categories. Similarities and differences in their perceptions of the search process were identified.

In addition, the data were analyzed within the context of the original model of the search process which had been developed in a prior study. Refinements and adjustments of the model were made.

Qualitative methods, such as longitudinal studies and case studies, are essential for filling the gaps that quantitative studies leave and for raising new questions and hypotheses that need to be further tested quantitatively. The two forms of research build a theory base through the opening and closing cycle of questioning and testing. Dervin and Nilan (1986, p. 27) state that traditional studies of information needs and uses have examined one discrete information incident rather than taking a more holistic view of information use. Longitudinal study, combined with case study, unlike the snapshot approach, has the power to reveal the complex cognitive process that takes place over a period of time involving the whole person, emotionally as well as intellectually, and so offers a holistic view of the search process.

## EMERGING THEORY OF A PROCESS APPROACH TO INFORMATION SEEKING

This chapter has described the methodology used for a series of research studies into user's perspective of information seeking. The methods were developed to reveal the experience of users within the search process investigating an extensive problem over a period of time. Both qualitative and quantitative methods were developed to build and verify a model of the Information Search Process. A combination of qualitative and quantitative methods provided over-lapping data that offered a comprehensive view of a complex, dynamic process. These studies initiate an area of research into the Information Search Process for further investigation, verification, and refinement.

The two main assumptions on which the methodology were based are that a longitudinal approach is necessary for studying the search process and that field studies are essential for eliciting real-life experience. The methods were developed to study real people with real problems in real libraries. Therefore, the methods are particu-larly appropriate for application as tools for action research in library and information systems. In addition, these methods were intended to open the search process for observation and may be adopted as process interventions to enable users to become aware of and to understand their own search process.

From the findings of these five studies on the Information Search Process viewed within the perspective of the constructivist theory of learning emerges a theory of a process approach to information seeking in library and information services. This emerging theory is articulated as a principle of uncertainty in the next chapter.

# Chapter 7

## Uncertainty Principle

This chapter proposes a theory for library and information services based on the constructivist view of learning and grounded in the findings of the series of studies in the Information Search Process of library users described in this book. We began with a borrowed theory, tested that theory within the context of information-seeking situations, and now proceed to make a theoretical statement specific to information-seeking behavior. When the borrowed theory was empirically examined within the frame of library users' experience, information seeking was revealed as a process of construction. The constructivist view could then be articulated as a theory for library and information services. A process theory is specifically articulated and proposed as a premise on which to base interventions with users of library and information systems.

A process theory for library and information services addressed a common experience of uncertainty and anxiety. Theory building is strengthened by expanding on a principle existing in the literature of the field. An uncertainty principle has been introduced into information science by several other researchers.

Bates (1986) recommends that uncertainty be used as one of three design principles, the others being variety and complexity. The mechanistic assumption is that there is an ideal indexing system with one perfect description of a document which will produce the best match with the user's information need and query. Bates maintains that the ideal is impossible in principle because of fundamental human traits which make indexing behavior and information searching behavior varied and individual. Therefore, a principle of uncertainty is posited to allow for the indeterminate range of mental associations that characterize human thought.

Whittemore and Yovits (1973) also propose an uncertainty principle for the fundamental theory of information flow. They summarize the three levels of communication research identified by Shannon and Weaver (1949) by posing three questions: "What is the message?," "What does the message mean?," and "What are the effects of the message on the recipient?" Concentrating on the third level, their research addresses the effectiveness and meaning of information to the user for decision making, referred to as pragmatic information. Addressing the problem of the way that information is used once it is transmitted and received, they set out to evaluate information in terms of the reduction of uncertainty for the decision maker. According to Shannon and Weaver (1949),

> Uncertainty is the critical link between information and decision-making. To effect a meaningful analysis of pragmatic information, one must look in detail at that which makes decision making such a challenging and oftentimes agonizing activity: uncertainty. (p. 224)

Uncertainty involved in decision making enlivens learning and makes selection into a dynamic process (Yovits and Foulk, 1985). As understanding of the situation changes over time, attitude toward uncertainty changes as well. In the decision-making process confidence increases as the person obtains results which he or she predicts;

> The confidence which the decision-maker has in his current model clearly affects the manner in which his state of knowledge is altered by the learning process and is an important factor in choosing a course of action. (p. 64)

Testing the premise that information always reduces uncertainty, Yovits and Foulk (1985) found that in some situations information may make a person more, not less, uncertain of his or her appraisal of a particular situation. They noted that typical decision models address those who are assumed to have reached a rather advanced state of knowledge about the decision situation in question. Information science, however, must cover all levels of decision making, novel situations in which a sequence of related decisions are required over a period of time as well as advanced decision situations.

Building on the recognition of the importance of uncertainty introduced by these researchers, the emerging theory is further developed and articulated. Research into the users' actual experience in the process of using information for seeking meaning, gaining a deeper understanding, and learning reveals pervasive patterns of uncertainty. Studies of the user's perspective of information seeking suggest an underlying persistence of uncertainty that describes and shapes the way that the process is commonly experienced. An uncertainty principle is proposed as a basic premise in the process of learning from information access and use.

## PERSONAL CONSTRUCT THEORY AS AN EXAMPLE OF THEORY BUILDING

Kelly's presentation of Personal Construct Theory offers a prototype for theory building which is composed of a fundamental postulate elaborated by a series of corollaries. The corollaries explain and elaborate the fundamental postulate but are not presented in any particular hierarchical or priority order.

By adopting Kelly's prototype, an uncertainty principle, based on the findings of the series of studies into the user's perspective of the information search process, is proposed. The central principle, as the fundamental postulate, is supported and expanded by six corollaries which are also drawn from the findings of the studies. The uncertainty principle is presented as a proposal for an emerging theory of intervention that is further developed and discussed in Chapters 8 and 9.

This theoretical statement is meant to stand alone as an underlying principle for the development of process-oriented library and information services. Some of the discussions may seem to reiterate concepts presented in Chapter 2 that discuss constructivist theory. This chapter, however, is a redefinition of constructivist theory as it directly applies to library and information services. The uncertainty principle is stated as a theoretical underpinning for the process approach to services.

## UNCERTAINTY PRINCIPLE

Uncertainty is a cognitive state that commonly causes affective symptoms of anxiety and lack of confidence. Uncertainty and anxiety can be expected in the early stages of the Information Search Process. The affective symptoms of uncertainty, confusion, and frustration are associated with vague, unclear thoughts about a topic or question. As knowledge states shift to more clearly focused thoughts, a parallel shift occurs in feelings of increased confidence. Uncertainty due to a lack of understanding, a gap in meaning, or a limited construct initiates the process of information seeking.

### Process Corollary

The process of information seeking involves construction in which the user actively pursues understanding and meaning from the information encountered over a period of time. The process is commonly experienced as a series of thoughts and feelings that shift from vague and anxious to clear and confident as the search progresses.

Users experience the active process of information seeking as a process of construction, much the way that the theorists have described. Dewey's phases of reflective experience, Kelly's phases of construction, and Bruner's interpretive task provide a theoretical basis for understanding individual experience in using information. The studies of the users' perspective described in Chapters 4 and 5 indicate that people commonly experience a series of phases or stages as they seek information over an extended period of time. Within the stages of the search process, people construct their own perspective or understanding of a topic or problem. The stages are experienced as an increase in understanding, interest, and confidence from the initiation to the conclusion of the process.

The process involves the total person and incorporates thinking, feeling, and acting in the dynamic process of learning. From the user's point of view, information seeking is a holistic experience with thoughts, actions, and feelings interweaving in a complex mosaic rather than as separate distinct entities. Thoughts unfold through actions and feelings evolve throughout. The holistic process of information seeking has not been fully supported in library and information services. While information seeking is recognized as a cognitive process, the affective process is rarely considered as interacting with the cognitive as part of a whole experience. Within the traditional bibliographic paradigm, we have attended almost exclusively to actions with location as the central objective. Recently, more consideration has been given to the cognitive aspects of information use with thinking and interpretation as a goal. Incorporation of the affective, however, is essential for fully understanding the experience of information seeking, but it has not yet occurred on any significant scale.

Information searching is traditionally portrayed as a systematic, orderly procedure rather than the uncertain, confusing process that users commonly experience. After the search is completed, the topic understood and the problem solved, it is all too easy to look back and deny the chaos and confusion that was actually experienced in the process. But, at what cost?

Bruner (1986) warned of a poverty bred by making too sharp a distinction among cognition, affect, and action, what he calls "tripartism." Consideration of all three in unison offers new approaches and insights to longstanding issues and problems in information provision.

The Information Search Process may not always be as clear-cut as the six-stage model might imply. The model is more of a metaphor for common experience in the search process than a prescription or a precise replication of individual experience. For example, the studies reported in this text examine problems with a distinct beginning and end. The beginning and end of the Information Search Process is often difficult to isolate and define. The level of the user's uncertainty, rather than the age of his or her problem, may be a better indicator of the point in the process that the user is experiencing. The concept of beginning and end is both fluid and elusive.

The expert may not experience uncertainty in the same way that the novice does. The expert is rarely at the true beginning as is a novice who holds only a few constructs on a topic. The expert in one area, however, may be a novice in another. Many doctoral students have identified with this process as matching their experience in dissertation research and writing. Practicing professionals have noted a similar process in preparing reports, lectures, sermons, briefs, papers, presentations, and articles.

The model of the Information Search Process is useful for describing a series of feelings and thoughts commonly related to the tasks in an evolving search process. However, the process is extremely complex, dynamic, and individual. The user's experience is complicated by two levels of process; the process of construction for meaning which overlays the process of information seeking. While the sequence of constructive experience described accurately emulates the search process, the pace of the process may vary greatly from individual to individual and search to search. The process may be more cyclical than the model implies, with stages recurring in a persistent quest for decreased uncertainty and increased understanding.

## Formulation Corollary

Formulation is thinking, developing an understanding, and extending and defining a topic from the information encountered in a search. The formulation of a focus or a guiding idea is a critical, pivotal point in a search when a general topic becomes clearer and a particular perspective is formed as the user moves from uncertainty to understanding.

Formulation, a central concept in this work, is thinking and forming thoughts during the process of a search. Understanding develops through extending and defining a topic from the information encountered. Thoughts change from vague and general to clear and specific. A personal perspective or point of view is formed from the information gathered. Formulation is based on former constructs and is, therefore, unique and personal. A consensus or an agreement may be made or some common ground established among information users, but this is not necessarily the expected outcome of information seeking.

The Information Search Process involves using information, not merely locating it. Using information involves interpreting and creating or, to adopt the phrase from Dewey and Bruner, "going beyond the information given." Formulation is the thinking that leads to interpreting and creating from the information encountered in the search process. The interpretive task, as Bruner described it, is critical to information seeking. No matter the amount or the quality of the information gathered, the problem is not solved or the topic understood until the information has been interpreted. The person actively creates possible alternative ways to interpret information in the process of seeking information.

Interpretation is highly individual. A group of people can pursue the same general topic or problem, and each come up with quite different perspectives and solutions. There is no one perfect paper as there is no one perfect formulation, interpretation, or creation. There are many ways to view the world, and many formulations contribute to our collective understanding. There is no one way out of uncertainty, but, rather, there is an individual process of construction within the Information Search Process. A certainty approach to information seeking, which promotes a single right answer to a specific question, obscures the central task of formulation for moving from uncertainty to understanding in complex issues.

The concept of formulation provides a way of understanding and articulating the user's task in the search process. In the study of the Information Search Process of users in three types of libraries, nearly 50 percent of the participants did not reach a focused topic at any point in their search process. In addition, most users identified their task as gathering and completing, even in the early stages of information seeking. The case studies provide an elaboration of the user's experience when very little formulation takes place during the process of the search. A lack of formulation resulted in significant writing blocks and great difficulty preparing to present the topic. One participant explained that when there was no focus, there was nothing to center on and nothing to complete; therefore, the paper was impossible to write. Formulation, as the central task in the search process, is frequently misunderstood by users and mediators alike.

Formulation of a focus is a critical pivotal point in a search when the general topic becomes clearer and a particular perspective is formed. Although the focus may be conceived of as a hypothesis, it may be quite tentative and fluid. A focus serves as a guiding idea that gives the search direction, narrows the search, and provides a basis for making relevance judgments. A focus may emerge slowly or be a sudden moment of insight. When little formulation has been made within the search process and no focus formed, difficulty is commonly experienced in writing and presenting the topic.

Disconcerting feelings are commonly associated with formulation. Users often find the period preceding formulation of a focus as the most difficult phase in the search process. Uncertainty commonly increases, rather than gradually decreasing, during this time. Users experience anxiety and frustration as they encounter information available from many different perspectives, much of which is not compatible with their own constructs. Some may be tempted to turn back and drop the quest altogether. We have no way of knowing just how many searches have been abandoned at this point. The connection between feelings and formulating is evident from the shift in increased confidence that parallels increased clarity as formulation unfolds.

Exploration is key for formulating a focus during the search process. However, users often move directly from selecting a general topic or area to the task of collecting information, skipping the important stage of exploration altogether. Exploratory acts uncover information for formulating new constructs, whereas collecting acts gather information for documenting established constructs. Formulation, which takes place through acting and reflecting, is more compatible with the task of exploring than that of collecting.

Tolerance for uncertainty is one of the important strategies for formulation within the search process. Some other practical strategies leading to formulation are talking, writing, browsing, reading, and reflecting. Mediators, frequently family and friends, play an important part in a person's formulation in the process of understanding information. Libraries and information systems, which have been devised primarily for collection rather than exploration, too often actually inhibit strategies that foster formulation. New forms of mediation that encourage and engage exploration are needed.

Kelly (1963) describes certain choices as elaborative, which leads to clarification or expansion and brings new understanding and direction. Elaborative choices in the process of information seeking give the search a focus or a theme enabling the user to move ahead with greater certainty and confidence toward closure. Such elaborative choices occur after considerable exploration and formulation have taken place. For example, a particular source may be seen as critical in triggering the formulation. However, if the source had been encountered earlier in the process it may have been considered relevant to the topic but not recognized as pertinent to the constructed focus. Formulation provides a framework for judging relevance of information. A shift may be noted, after a focus has been formed, from seeking information that is relevant to the general topic to wanting information that is pertinent to the focused perspective of the individual. The formulation of a focus is an elaborative choice that moves the search from uncertainty to understanding.

## Redundancy Corollary

The interplay of seeking what is expected or redundant and encountering what is unexpected or unique results in an underlying tension in the search process. Redundant information fits into what we already know and is promptly recognized as being either relevant or irrelevant. Unique information does not match our constructs and requires reconstruction to be recognized as useful. Redundancy may be expected to increase as uncertainty decreases. The lack of redundancy at the beginning of the search process may be an underlying cause of anxiety related to uncertainty.

The significant impact of emotion on the constructive process of information seeking is illustrated by the problem of redundancy versus uniqueness encountered in a search. Redundancy is that information which fits into what we already know and is promptly recognized as being relevant to our topic. Uniqueness is that information which does not match our former constructs and prompts us to construct new ideas and learn new concepts. The interplay of seeking what is expected or redundant on the one hand and encountering what is unexpected or unique on the other is little understood within the Information Search Process.

Redundancy in new information verifies what we know. Uniqueness in new information adds to what we know. The balance of redundancy and uniqueness is critical in a search for information. Too much redundancy results in boredom; too much uniqueness causes anxiety. There is a distinct linkage between emotion and thinking which bears upon the actions that we take and the choices that we make. Relaxing and a tolerance for the learning process seem to be important for comfortable progression. However, as the Yerkes-Dodson Law reminds us, while too much tension causes one to spin wheels, too little causes one to loose interest.

The individual information user does not treat all information equally. Rather, a person selectively attends to certain aspects of the information encountered and ignores others. Selective attending patterns do not remain stable throughout a search but change and evolve as understanding increases.

In this way, the balance of redundancy and uniqueness shifts during the stages of the Information Search Process. Early in the process the amount of uniqueness is likely to be much greater than later in the process. At the beginning, familiar information or redundancy is a reassuring sign that there is something that fits in with what we already know and that we are on the right track. Uncertainty and anxiety can be expected as a result of the large amount of uniqueness encountered. Tolerance for uniqueness, that which does not fit with our constructs, is essential in the early stages. Toward the midpoint of the Information Search Process, some of the initial uniqueness takes on meaning as we build new constructs. At this point, thoughts become clearer and more focused and selections of relevance become more pertinent and to the point. At the end of the process, the amount of redundancy in the information encountered and gathered can be expected to be much greater than the amount of uniqueness. Much of the initial uniqueness has been reconstructed into the familiar. The shift to encountering mostly redundant information lessens anxiety and raises confidence.

There is much we do not know about how individuals construe and reconstrue during information seeking. These studies do indicate, however, that the process is not purely cognitive. Feelings of anxiety are prevalent early in the search, and levels of confidence increase considerably during the process.

There are different degrees in the amount of information that can be understood at different stages in the process. Therefore, information overload is a relative, not a stable, concept. An understanding of the affective aspects of the search process seems to result in a tolerance for stages that commonly cause discomfort. One of the case study subjects in a recent interview noted that he never can have too much information because he has learned to tolerate uniqueness and the feeling of uncertainty that accompanies more information than can easily be assimilated or reconstructed at one time. The studies of the search process of users indicate that an understanding of the feelings commonly experienced and a tolerance for the anxiety commonly associated with uncertainty are important concepts for users to have. A misreading of feelings as a signal of failure is likely to occur when users do not have an understanding of the affective component of the constructive process of information seeking.

## Mood Corollary

Mood, a stance or attitude that the user assumes, opens or closes the range of possibilities in a search. An invitational mood leads to expansive actions, while an indicative mood leads to conclusive actions. The user's mood may be expected to shift during the search process. An invitational mood may be more appropriate for the early stages of the search, and an indicative mood more appropriate for the latter stages.

One critical way that emotion affects the process of information seeking is by the stance or mood that the user assumes. A mood may be thought of as an attitude which determines one's approach to the task at hand. Kelly (1963) describes two moods in any constructive process, one is invitational and the other indicative.

Assuming a single mood, either invitational or indicative, throughout the entire Information Search Process may obstruct progress at certain points. The ability to alter mood as the search progresses allows for the accommodation of the different tasks in each of the various stages.

At Initiation, an invitational mood tends to open the possibilities within the confines of the comprehensive topic or problem and keeps at bay any tendency toward early closure based on insufficient information. At Selection, however, when the task is to choose the general direction or topic, a more indicative stance prompts the decision to be made. When users are overly invitational, at this point, they are likely to have difficulty settling on a general topic in order to get their search underway. On the other hand, when they are excessively indicative they tend to choose topics without sufficient investigation and reflection which frequently result in obstacles later on. At the Exploration stage, an invitational mood opens the search for accomplishing the task of investigating and learning about the general topic. An indicative mood at this point prompts the person to collect rather than to explore. In this time of extension, a productive strategy is to relax, read, and reflect, and to list ideas rather than to take copious notes. At the Formulation stage, an indicative mood fosters the closure essential to accomplish the task of narrowing and focusing the general problem area. The indicative mood is also effective in the Collection stage when the task centers on gathering information specific to the focused perception of the topic. The indicative mood aids the user to seek closure in preparation for presenting the information during the last stage, Presentation.

In general, the invitational mood is likely to be most effective in the earlier stages of the search process, and the indicative mood is more appropriate for the tasks at and after midpoint. An invitational mood throughout may result in a lack of focus and closure. An indicative mood throughout may result in a lack of new construction and learning. The ability to shift stance to match the task at hand during the search process is a strategy of experienced searchers.

The question of whether moods assumed by users are actually styles that persist across searches is important to consider. Are moods attitudes that may be easily changed, or styles with persistent patterns of habits? The studies did reveal evidence of styles that users assumed, however the styles did not seem so fixed that they could not be adjusted when the users became aware of them as a result of extensive search experience.

The case study participants were examined for research styles which persisted over time. It was noted that two case studies showed evidence of more invitational mood tendencies and two showed evidence of tendencies that could be identified as more indicative. During their high school information-seeking situations these tendencies impeded their process at the points in the search, as described above. Those displaying invitational mood tendencies had difficulty in selecting topics, forming focuses, and closing the search for presentation. Those with indicative tendencies tended to choose topics without sufficient preliminary investigation and to focus without forming constructs from the information they encountered. The tendency toward one style was modified during college to accommodate both invitational and indicative moods so as to better address the tasks of the different stages of the search process.

The bibliographic paradigm projects an image of the task of

information seeking that is primarily to gather and collect information rather than be a series of tasks within a constructive process. In
this way, the traditional approach to information seeking fosters an
indicative mood. A misconception of tasks seems to pervade users'
understanding of what they are about in information-seeking situations. In the study of the users in three types of libraries, described
in Chapter 5, the one area of responses that did not match the model
of users' experience in the search process related to perception of a
changing task throughout the process. The model describes the
following series of tasks:

- Initiation—to recognize information need;
- Selection—to identify general topic;
- Exploration—to investigate information on general topic;
- Formulation—to formulate a focus;
- Collection—to gather information pertaining to the focus;
  and
- Presentation—to complete information search.

The users in the study choose "to gather and complete" from a list of
tasks for all stages in the search process. They did not identify any of
the other less indicative tasks for the earlier, more invitational stages
of the process, even though they reported experiencing these stages
differently.

In light of this finding, mediators may expect users to be impatient
with the more invitational aspects of information seeking. They feel
they are procrastinating when they reflect in the early phases of
construction. They have a tendency to move from selection to
collection, leaping over the critical invitational stages of exploration
in preparation for formulation. They use indicative strategies, such
as copious notetaking, when more invitational tactics, such as listing
interesting ideas, would be more appropriate. An exclusively indicative approach to information seeking is in conflict with the actual
experience of users.

**Prediction Corollary**

The search process may be thought of as a series of choices based on
predictions of what will happen if a particular action is taken.

Predictions are based on expectations derived from constructs built on past experience. Since each of us constructs our own unique personal worlds, the predictions and choices made in the search process may vary widely from user to user. Predictions may change during the search process, as the user moves from uncertainty to understanding.

One of the basic principles of construction theory is that each of us constructs our own unique personal worlds. When two people encounter similar information, the interpretation each makes may be quite different. Kelly (1963) explains this as happening through prediction based on personal constructs. "Individuals form constructs with which to predict future events" (p. 14). Since no two people hold precisely the same constructs, the predictions underlying their actions may vary widely.

In Kelly's terms, the predictions that users make during a search direct the information-gathering process. Only the action is observable. The underlying prediction remains hidden unless brought to the surface by a question or other intrusive probe.

Predictions are based on an expectation of what will happen if a certain action is taken, "If I choose this, this is likely to happen." Predictions can be wrong when they are not based on solid evidence. For example, the latest incident may be used rather than the accumulation of all that is known.

The concept of predicting outcome brings insight to the issue of relevance judgments. Relevance is not absolute and cannot be considered as constant from person to person. Choices within the search process are unique to the individual and may be expected to vary considerably. The most stable characteristic of relevance judgments is that they are not uniform. For this reason objective measurements of accuracy of information retrieval do not suffice for determining effective performance.

The search process involves a series of choices of what users find relevant or irrelevant. Kelly (1963) states that a person chooses that which will extend and define his or her system. In the process of a search users seek information that will extend and define the topic or problem. As constructs related to the topic being investigated in the search process are formed and clarified, choices of what information will extend and define also change. What was relevant at the beginning of a search may not be relevant later, and information not considered relevant early on may become pertinent in the later stages. To better understand the predictions that drive choices, it may be necessary to elicit what was rejected as well as what was accepted and why the choice was made.

Users predict, from constructs formed through prior experience, what will be useful and expedient in information seeking. The predictions determine the sources used, the sequence in which they are used, and the information that is gleaned from the sources. Conversely, user predictions determine information, sources, and even the ideas that remain or are discarded. This is a highly individual process based on one's system of personal constructs.

Predictions are made about topics and information related to topics but predictions are also made about process. Expectations are formed through the holistic experience of information seeking. Therefore, personal constructs relate not only to the cognitive aspects of the process but also to the affective experience in the search process. Feelings of anxiety at the beginning of a search affect the choices that one makes as do feelings of confidence in later stages. Predictions of outcome vary depending on where the user is in the process.

The four criteria for choices discussed earlier shed some light on how a person's expectations affect decisions made in the process of information seeking. The studies discussed in previous chapters identify the criteria of personal interest, assignment requirements, information available, and time allotted as important concerns in making choices during a search. In the Selection stage, people weigh potential topics against these criteria, predict outcomes of possible choices, and choose a topic with potential for success. In the Formulation stage users predict outcome using the same four criteria, but at this point they use the criteria to form a focus for completing the search task.

**Interest Corollary**

Interest increases as the exploratory inquiry leads to formulation in the Information Search Process. Motivation and intellectual engagement intensify along with construction. Personal interest may be expected to increase as uncertainty decreases.

Although an invitational mood seems to match the early stages in the search process and an indicative mood matches the later stages, there is another element of the information seeking experience closely related to mood. Interest is an important factor throughout the search process in these studies. Individual interest was reported to increase after the formulation of a focus. When construction was well underway and the topic was personally understood, users responded that they had become more interested in the topic or problem. This finding indicates that motivation resulting from personal interest is more pronounced after the midpoint of the search than at the beginning. It takes some time to become intellectually engaged in the topic of a search. The image of "hitting the ground running" is not descriptive of the search process from the user's perspective. Rather, the image of a gradual exploratory inquiry leading to discovery is a more accurate depiction, with interest increasing along with construction.

Dewey (1934) explains the influence of interest in learning by differentiating between the quality of a whole experience and that of an incomplete experience. A whole experience is an interaction of emotions and ideas in which conscious intent emerges. All experience is not consistently satisfying however. Sometimes there are

> distractions and dispersion; what we observe and what we think, what we desire and what we get, are at odds with each other. We put our hands to the plow and turn back; we start and then we stop, not because the experience has reached the end for the sake of which it was initiated but because of extraneous interruptions or of inner lethargy. In contrast with such experience, we have *an* experience when the material experienced runs its course to fulfillment. Then and only then is it integrated within and demarcated in the general stream of experience from other experiences. A piece of work is finished in a way that is satisfactory; a problem receives its solution; . . . a situation . . . is so rounded out that its close is a consummation and not a cessation. Such an experience is a whole and carries with it its own individualizing quality and self-sufficiency. (p. 35)

A whole experience is one in which intrinsic motivation directs the individual's action toward a satisfying conclusion.

Another factor in influencing interest in information seeking is the notion of fun and play. All creative pursuits have an element of fun, enjoyment, and pleasure. Work and play merge in a fully satisfying, creative experience. While some users profess an enjoyment in searching, in general aspects of drudgery and boredom are also evident. Bates (1986) asserts that information retrieval systems should be fun. The creative process of learning from information should be pleasurable. We overlook an essential human element by not investigating the play aspect of information seeking.

A number of researchers have studied motivation, investigating the explanations underlying the Yerkes-Dodson Law, which reveals the relation between intensity of motivation and level of learning (Biggs, 1976; Entwistle, 1981; Marton and Saljo, 1976; Pask, 1976). Under the direction of Marton, a group of researchers at the Institute of Education at the University of Gothenberg, Sweden, have made some important findings in this area. Fransson (1984), in an extensive series of studies on intrinsic and extrinsic motivation, found that interest plays a significant part in determining whether a person adopts a surface learning strategy or a deep learning strategy. Extrinsically motivated learners have higher levels of anxiety than do intrinsically motivated learners. According to Fransson,

> The conclusion to be drawn for teaching is that if deep-level processing is valued, every effort must be made to avoid threatening conditions, which rely mainly on extrinsic motivation. This is especially important when the initial level of interest of the students in the learning task is low. (Fransson, 1984, p. 115)

Perhaps similar implications may be drawn for mediation into the Information Search Process, particularly at initial points when level of interest in the task may be relatively low. This opens a fruitful area of research for investigating the relation of interest and anxiety in information-seeking situations.

## SUMMARY OF THE UNCERTAINTY PRINCIPLE

Uncertainty is a cognitive state that commonly causes affective symptoms of anxiety and lack of confidence. Uncertainty and anxiety can be expected in the early stages of the Information Search Process. The affective symptoms of uncertainty, confusion, and frustration are associated with vague, unclear thoughts about a topic or question. As knowledge states shift to more clearly focused thoughts, a parallel shift occurs in feelings of increased confidence. Uncertainty due to a lack of understanding, a gap in meaning, or a limited construct initiates the process of information seeking.

## Process Corollary

The process of information seeking involves construction in which the user actively pursues understanding and meaning from the information encountered over a period of time. The process is commonly experienced in a series of thoughts and feelings that shift from vague and anxious to clear and confident, as the search progresses.

## Formulation Corollary

Formulation is thinking, developing an understanding, and extending and defining a topic from the information encountered in a search. The formulation of a focus or a guiding idea is a critical, pivotal point in a search when a general topic becomes clearer and a particular perspective is formed as the user moves from uncertainty to understanding.

## Redundancy Corollary

The interplay of seeking what is expected or redundant and encountering what is unexpected or unique results in an underlying tension of the search process. Redundant information fits into what we already know and is promptly recognized as being relevant or irrelevant. Unique information does not match our constructs and requires reconstruction to be recognized as useful. Redundancy may be expected to increase as uncertainty decreases. The lack of redundancy at the beginning of the search process may be an underlying cause of anxiety related to uncertainty.

## Mood Corollary

Mood, a stance or attitude that the user assumes, opens or closes the range of possibilities in a search. An invitational mood leads to expansive actions while an indicative mood leads to conclusive actions. The user's mood may shift during the search process. An invitational mood may be more appropriate for the early stages of the search, and an indicative mood more appropriate for the latter stages.

## Prediction Corollary

The search process may be thought of as a series of choices based on predictions of what will happen if a particular action is taken. Predictions are based on expectations derived from constructs built on past experience. Since each of us constructs our own unique personal worlds, the predictions and choices made in the search process may vary widely from user to user. Predictions may be expected to change during the search process as the user moves from uncertainty to understanding.

## Interest Corollary

Interest increases as the exploratory inquiry leads to formulation in the Information Search Process. Motivation and intellectual engagement intensify along with construction. Personal interest may be expected to increase as uncertainty decreases.

## FROM UNCERTAINTY TO UNDERSTANDING

The uncertainty principle and the six corollaries propose a theoretical view of users in their search for information to gain understanding. Figure 7–1 compares the transition from uncertainty to understanding on three levels of experience: thinking, feeling, and acting. Uncertainty, at the initiation of the Information Search Process, is

|   | uncertainty ---------------------------------understanding | |
|---|---|
| T | vague | clear |
| F | anxious | confident |
| A | exploring | documenting |

**FIG. 7–1.  From Uncertainty to Understanding**

characterized by vague thoughts, anxious feelings, and exploratory actions. Understanding, later in the process, is characterized by clear thoughts, confident feelings, and documentary actions.

Mediation based on the bibliographic paradigm ignores the holistic view of information seeking as experienced by the user. Intervention is limited to actions for collecting and documenting. Mediation based on an uncertainty principle incorporates cognition, affect, and action from the user's perspective. Intervention encompasses actions for exploring and formulating. While it may not be necessary to dwell on feelings in information-seeking situations, it is necessary to incorporate an awareness of affect into our professional construct of information seeking. Until the triad of thinking, feeling, and acting is fully accepted as the nature of information seeking, mediation is likely to be fragmented and limited. The uncertainty principle is proposed as a basis for mediation into the process of learning from access to information, thereby enabling users to move from uncertainty to understanding.

# Chapter 8

## Roles of Mediators in the Process of Information Seeking

The uncertainty principle provides the basis for a process approach to intervening with users of libraries and information systems. Before exploring the ways that mediation might assist the search process, it is helpful to be aware of users' perceptions of the role of mediators, in general, and librarians, in particular. The studies of the search process revealed the role of both formal and informal mediators. The term mediator, rather than intermediary, is used for human intervention to assist information seeking and learning from information access and use. An intermediary intercedes between the information and the user but this interchange need not involve any human interaction. A mediator, however, implies a person who assists, guides, enables, and otherwise intervenes in another person's information search process.

### USERS' PERCEPTION OF THE ROLE OF MEDIATORS

In each of the studies of the user's perspective of information seeking, data were collected on the participants' perception of the role of mediators during completion of their information-seeking tasks. These studies identified two types of mediators, formal and informal. Formal mediators are professionals employed in the information system, such as librarians, and in the case of students, professors and teachers. Informal mediators are other people whom users talk to about their work, including family, friends, colleagues, and subject experts.

The findings of the studies, reported in this book, regardless of whether the library users were in an academic, public, or school library, revealed a limited role for formal mediators. The longitudinal studies further verified a limited, insignificant role for librarians attributed by users. The librarians, in most cases, were considered primarily organizers of the resources and sometimes given the role of a locator.

The high school students in the initial study (Kuhlthau, 1983), did not consider librarians to be major contributors to accomplishment of their information-seeking tasks. Constructs of the role of the librarian in their search process were very restricted. When asked if they need the librarian's assistance when researching a topic, only 3 of the 25 students responded either "almost always," or "often." When asked if they request help before choosing a topic, the students' responses indicated that this type of assistance was not considered to be the librarian's role. None of the students responded that they "almost always" or "often" ask the librarian for help before choosing a topic. Even after choosing a topic, most of the students did not "almost always" or even "often" seek a librarian's assistance. The students lacked constructs that would prompt them to request mediation from a librarian in even the more traditional tasks of topic selection and information collection. They regarded the library as based on self-service access with little provision for professional/ client interaction.

The verification study (Kuhlthau, Turock, George, and Belvin, 1990) of three types of library users, which included 385 people, also revealed a limited use of librarians during information seeking. One of the items on a questionnaire, "Who have you talked to about your project?," sought to uncover those who were perceived as mediators during the search process. This question may not have revealed who actually was employed as a mediator, but it did show participants' perceptions of who served that function for them. The following four categories were used: friend or family member, peer (one doing a similar task), expert (teacher, professor, or one who knows about the topic), or professional (librarian). Responses indicated that 39% of the respondents consulted experts, 25% conferred with librarians,

20% reported using friends and family, and 13% talked with peers. There was no significant change during the search process nor was there a significant difference by type of library. Although librarians were a group with whom all of the participants in this study had direct contact, they were not identified in 75% of the responses. A wide range of experts was mentioned, however, drawing from the community and other contacts.

The case studies (Kuhlthau, 1988c) verified the limited role and disclosed a perception of the librarian as a "last resort" source locator. The librarian was described as a person to go to when you are "stuck." One person explained that when he is "totally stuck," he asks a librarian and expects to be directed to a specific source. Another student stated that the librarian helps with "obscure sources, like how to use law books." And, another related that if "I can't find something, I guess I try to find the easy way out and ask the librarian." Seeking assistance from the librarian was seen as taking the "easy way out" and not as a legitimate approach to researching a topic or as an integral part of the search process.

## THE ROLE OF FORMAL MEDIATORS

Although the role of the librarian was considered as insignificant, the participants frequently turned to informal mediators, including parents, siblings, and friends. Many students considered talking about their topics as an important strategy both during and after topic selection. In the original study, only 5 students replied that they "seldom" or "almost never" discuss their topic in the process of selection. After they have chosen their topic, even more students responded that they talk about it with another person or used an informal mediator. Only one responded "seldom" and none of the students stated that they "almost never" discuss their topic. Although many of the students felt a need to discuss their topic selection and the development of ideas with others, they did not consider talking about the development of their topics with the librarian. Most of the students revealed that they expected (or were expected) to proceed totally on their own without assistance from formal mediators. They perceived that librarians had little or no role in their search process.

The case study subjects further explained that they wanted to discuss their topics with another person and that they sought help in thinking through some of the ideas that they confronted in the search process. For this help they frequently turned to informal mediators. One related a way that his father assisted him in formulating a focus;

> I showed him what I was doing and he would be able to guide me. He would actually help me to organize it. He'd take out a piece of paper and say 'OK, these are the ways you are headed, now which one do you want.' He would just lay it out for me, but he would try not to influence me.

The study revealed that students attributed a limited, source-oriented role to librarians while they frequently reported making use of a variety of informal mediators in the process of their library research. The case studies confirmed the view of the librarian's role as very limited and source-oriented. The librarian's role was described as directing them to sources that they had difficulty locating on their own. Some students warned that too much assistance might in some way spoil the project by making it less than their own work. Informal mediators assisted students by listening, offering encouragement, and sometimes recommending a strategy. Although the students were seeking guidance in formulation, they wanted the important decisions about the project to remain with them.

## CALL FOR FORMAL MEDIATION INTO PROCESS OF INFORMATION SEEKING

The students seemed to recognize their own needs for help and seek process intervention from informal mediators. They frequently discussed thoughts that they were forming about their topic with informal mediators, but they seldom mentioned the specific sources that they were using. At the end of the study, the case study participants expressed a need for an expanded process-oriented role for the formal mediator, either the teacher or the librarian. The students also reveal confusion between the role of the teacher and of the librarian as formal mediators. Each participant described a desire for guidance with the process of the search, as well as with the sources of information. The following are examples of the statements from case study subjects made in response to the question, "What further help could you have used?"

One person said:

> Encouragement. Being able to go to the teacher and say, "This is my topic what do you think." I don't know if anyone did that. I did it with friends, but friends don't know what the possibilities are . . . They don't know what information is available. You could say to the librarian, "This is my topic. Do you think I could find enough information? Where should I go?" That would help at the beginning.

This person's statement, although primarily source-oriented, first and foremost seeks encouragement. When asked how a mediator might be helpful she responded without hesitation, "encouragement." Acknowledgement of the uncertainty and encouraging support are primary features of process-oriented mediation. Second, the statement reveals a need or at least an inclination to talk about the topic with someone. Conversation and dialogue facilitate formulation and are important elements in any constructive process. Third, is the realization that informal mediators have a limited capacity for help and that formal mediators provide professional guidance.

Another student's statement regarding further help reveals even more need for the introduction of mediation in the search process. A participant explained,

> You have a research paper. It's due in four weeks . . . It's all on your own; I guess, research papers are. . . . They could have done something in between; given us ideas. Teachers are so nonchalant about giving research papers. . . . They don't discuss it with you . . . In the meantime, the teacher isn't really being there. I don't think they should say 'Let me see your notecards.' But they should say, 'Ok, tomorrow we'll talk about what you found, if you have any problems, or what point you are at.' Not pressure you, 'Well if you haven't started just forget it.' Sometimes you haven't started because you don't know what you're about. It would help to know if everyone else was lost, too.

Within this person's statement is a clear call for process mediation, the need for someone "being there" during the process. "Being there" is further described as including the following: Intervention to address what you have found, any problems you may have, and the point you are at in the process.

Both of these people were groping for some formal mediation, beyond mere location of sources, into the process of their search. They indicated a need for more help at the beginning of the process. In the collection stage, after a problem has been well-defined and formulated, the library system works fairly efficiently. After most of the uncertainty has been resolved the system functions effectively. But, these people seemed to be calling out for help in the midst of the uncertainty and confusion of the earlier stages.

Process mediation would provide opportunities to "talk about" ideas as they emerge. A process approach would acknowledge common experience of uncertainty in the early stages of the process. There is a need for process mediation because such mediation does not increase anxiety by "pressuring you" into premature closure. Caution is recommended against overly indicative intervention, such as the traditional requirement of a thesis statement and outline before the exploration and formulation necessary for collection and closure. There is a call for more invitational intervention, such as dialogue for clarifying emerging ideas, which fosters exploration and formulation. It is in these early stages of the search process that traditional mediation is at its weakest.

## PROVIDING INFORMATION FOR THE PROCESS OF CONSTRUCTION

Scrutiny of these statements of users reveals a need for mediation addressing two major aspects of information seeking, access to sources and guidance in process. Although this work concentrates on the process of information seeking, that is not to suggest that help with sources of information is unnecessary. The two types of mediation are connected and interrelated in subtle ways. The structure, sequence, format, and depth of information are critical considerations when access to sources is placed within the context of the Information Search Process.

### Product and Process

There is a need to give attention to the product verses process debate, which differentiates between help with sources and help with process. Information-related mediation assists with access to information. Process-related mediation assists with learning from the use of information. Uncertainty underlies both product and process and is likely to be compounded in actual situations of information seeking. While not the focus of this research, source and product also factor in uncertainty. The tension between process and product needs to be addressed in mediation.

Uncertainty, which can be caused by a lack of ability to find needed information, is inherent in the process of learning from information access and use. Studies by Mellon (1986) show that anxiety is prevalent when students are required to use a library that is unfamiliar to them. Users' perceptions of quantity as well as their perceptions of ignorance seem to factor in their uncertainty. Perceptions of quantity relate to the physical environment. The sheer size of the facility and collection is often overwhelming and inhibiting. Perceptions of ignorance relate to a sense of not knowing how to find information, of not knowing what sources are available, and of the expectation that everyone should know how to do a library search.

There are two aspects to mediation; one is information-related, which leads to access to information and sources, and the other is process-related, which leads to problem solving and learning. There is a need to develop strategies for intervening with users; these strategies should incorporate both increased access and enhanced process. The primary concentration of this work, however, is on more innovative process intervention, although some consideration has been given to increased access as well.

**Structure and Sequence**

Information does not serve the same function in all of the phases of the Information Search Process. It follows that for information to be most useful it needs to be presented in ways that match the user's cognitive and affective level.

Bruner's (1973) three basic considerations for learning are: the nature of the knowledge to be learned, the nature of the knower, and the nature of the knowledge-getting process. Up to this point, we have been concentrating on the nature of the knowledge-getting process. In addition, the nature of the knowledge to be learned and the nature of the knower or learner need to be considered for providing mediation into the search process.

Structuring a discipline for learning is based on the idea that "any subject can be taught to any person at any age in some form that is honest" (Bruner, 1977, p. 33). To facilitate learning, subject matter and format must be sequenced to present concepts and information meaningfully. Thus, Bruner recommended a spiral curriculum, building on a concept introduced by Dewey some years before, which starts where the learner is, uses the mode of thinking that he or she possesses, and makes knowledge accessible to the learner as a problem solver. This concept underlies the practice of recommending paths through a collection of information and suggesting a sequence for encountering and gathering the information.

Piaget's (Inhelder and Piaget, 1958) work on cognitive development also has some insights into the issue of sequencing information. Piaget describes children as progressing through a series of stages of cognitive development, with their capacity for the abstract increasing with age. The young concrete thinker may have difficulty dealing in more abstract concepts. Since many aspects of information seeking require considerable skill in abstraction, there is a need to accommodate tasks to the individual level of cognitive development.

Piaget described cognitive development in a series of stages which may be thought of as a continuum rather than strict locked steps (Elkind, 1976). His work provides an understanding of the person's natural way of thinking at different stages of development. His stages are sensorimotor, preoperational, concrete operational, and formal operational. Piaget used the term operational for the ability to internalize action and for the mental operation of getting data about the world, and of organizing and selecting data in the solution of problems. Formal operational thinking develops sometime between the ages of 11 and 16 and provides the person with the mental tools for abstract problem solving and independent learning. The formal operational person can use abstract thought and deductive reasoning. Thought is more flexible, rational, and systematic. The person can solve problems by searching for a solution in a systematic fashion using alternative ways from several points of view—all of which are basic skills of information seeking.

## Format and Depth

Bruner (1975) extends Piaget's stages of cognitive development to encompass all learners depending on their point in the learning process, their prior experience and knowledge, as well as their stage of cognitive development. Enactive, the earliest stage, is acting within a concrete experience and learning from that interaction. Iconic, one step removed from the actual concrete experience, is visualization within a vicarious experience. Symbolic, the third stage, is using verbal and written symbols to learn and think. Learning moves through the stages of enactive, iconic, and symbolic as the learner's knowledge and level of understanding deepens.

When these stages are placed within the context of the stages of the Information Search Process, we begin to see patterns for information presentation. During Initiation and Selection, enactive information may increase understanding of the concrete aspects of the problem and provide a personal connection. During Exploration, iconic information may provide a vicarious experience on which to build abstract dimensions. During Formulation and Collection, symbolic information may extend abstract thinking grounded in a deep personal understanding. Dale's (1969) cone of experience, which depicts where various types of media might fall within Bruner's three categories of experience, serves to illustrate how information may be sequenced by format. For example, enactive media would include exhibits, field trips, demonstrations; iconic media would include television, film, recordings, and pictures; and abstract media would include all printed materials. Although somewhat dated, the underlying concept might be applied to emerging computer and video technologies.

Two aspects to the presentation of information need to be recognized. One is the format of the information, or the medium or the package in which the information is presented to the user. The other is the depth of the information in terms of subject matter content. The concrete to abstract continuum addresses both format of presentation and depth of presentation. While we may be tempted to view the format/depth issue in a simplistic way, at closer scrutiny, the complexity of the issue becomes obvious. All iconic presentations are not of equal depth. Some films are unquestionably more abstract than others. Of course, symbolic presentations vary in a similar way.

Unfortunately, there is no simple chart for sequencing information into the search process of users. What can be offered is a challenge to information professionals to consider the concrete to abstract continuum and the connections between format and depth in interventions that sequence information in a meaningful way.

Different ways of knowing fit different levels of knowing. The information rich environment of our technological age offers constant access to diverse formats of information in our everyday lives. Understanding the interrelationship of different information media is a critical element in interacting with information users. Many of the more pervasive media are enactive and iconic. How does the organized collection which is primarily symbolic connect with other ways of knowing? Mediation is essential to enable people to make connections, to move from concrete to abstract, to recognize the need to know more, to dig deeper, and to gain greater understanding.

## LEVELS OF MEDIATION

There are a number of levels of intervention and various forms of mediation into the information-seeking behavior of users. Librarians and the systems they have designed have been quite useful for intervention in the later stages of the process after formulation has taken place. At that point in the process, users can articulate fairly clearly what they are looking for and the information system can respond consistently and directly. The system has, in fact, been designed for just this sort of intervention. It is when we get into the more murky waters at the early stages that the system does not respond as well.

From the librarian's point of view, there are a variety of roles or relations to the user which must be recognized in order to choose an appropriate level of intervention. Within reference service, five levels of mediation have been identified: Level 1, the Organizer; Level 2, the Locator; Level 3, the Identifier; Level 4, the Advisor; and Level 5, the Counselor (see Figure 8-1). For each level, the chapter discusses the type of intervention and underlying assumptions related to the bibliographic paradigm or the uncertainty principle. Information seeking is addressed within the frame of reference of the model of the search process. The level of mediation is discussed in terms of the user's stage

| | Level | Description |
|---|---|---|
| 1 | Organizer | No Intervention<br>self service search in an organized collection |
| 2 | Locator | Ready Reference Intervention<br>single fact or source search;<br>query/answer |
| 3 | Identifier | Standard Reference Intervention<br>subject search;<br>group of sources in no particular order;<br>problem/interview/sources |
| 4 | Advisor | Pattern Intervention<br>subject search;<br>group of sources in recommended order;<br>problem/negotiation/sequence |
| 5 | Counselor | Process Intervention<br>constructive search;<br>holistic experience;<br>problem/dialogue/strategy/sources/sequence<br>redefinition |

**FIG. 8–1.  Levels of Mediation**

in the process and the complexity of the user's problem. Possible
search strategies for each level of mediation are noted.

## Level 1: Organizer

At Level 1, Organizer, no direct intervention is provided. Many
possible interventions do not include direct human contact. The
system as intermediary encompasses everything from the arrange-
ment of the facility, the signs and directions, accessibility of materials, the organization of indexes and catalogs, and all of these
factors in relation to advanced technology. The other levels of
mediation, however, are intended to address human intervention
with a library or other information system. The collection of
resources is made available through a system of classification and
through catalogs and indexes. No differentiation is made among
sources with the exception of subject classification and identification
of format. Physical access is indicated inhouse or from remote
locations. In this case, the role of the librarian is to provide an
organized collection of resources.

The underlying assumption of Level 1 is firmly grounded in the bibliographic paradigm and is based on a concept of certainty rather than uncertainty. The Organizer's ultimate task is to collect and organize sources and to maintain the collection for efficient retrieval. Total attention is given to sources and technology. The individual user and the individual's problem are peripheral to the Organizer's primary responsibility and concern.

Access to the collection is through a self-service search which the user conducts, often without human intervention through a system of classification. Access is available to the total collection, all at once, all the time. This is the commonest use of libraries and databases. An individual comes to the collection with a topic or problem, with the intent of collecting sources related or remotely related. The index gives rudimentary information on sources, such as format, citation, and classification. Little human intervention occurs with the possible exception of the transaction at the circulation desk. No mediation into the intellectual process of the user takes place. The effectiveness of this level depends on the users' proficiency in the search and on the complexity of the problem under investigation. Later stages in the search process are more suited to the Organizer level than are the early stages.

The Organizer's role, however, underlies all of the other levels of mediation. Without the Organizer there would be no collection of resources to access for learning or for any other purposes. The demands of the Organizer's role, however, have tended to consume the librarian and to overshadow the importance of the other levels of mediation for increasing access and guiding use.

## Level 2: Locator

Level 2, Locator, offers what is traditionally called ready reference intervention, when the user has a clear, simple question. A single fact or item search is conducted and the answer or the source is provided. The principle underlying this type of mediation is that there is a right answer and a single right source that will match the user's question; "Tell me what you want and I can give it to you." Information is treated as a thing or product that can be produced or provided.

The underlying assumption of the Locator level is that the system is certain, that questions are simple, and that there is one right answer. The concept of accuracy as a measure of outcome of service fits this level of mediation. Many of the accountability measures for reference service have been built on this concept. How many questions can be answered in an afternoon or evening at the reference desk? The more the better. "Quickly, tell me your question and I will locate the answer," is the synopsis of this reference approach, a single incident, a simple question, and a matched source.

Locator mediation may include a range of interventions from a directive to use a specific tool for locating sources, such as a catalog or an index, or the location of a specific answer to a specific question. The user may be present at the reference desk or at a terminal, or the user may be at a remote location on the phone or in another office down the hall. The Locator's responses may range from a mere gesture indicating a direction to a search looking up an item and giving the answer. In most instances, a source is located in response to a specific request.

The Locator is effective for simple, straightforward, single-issue questions. Although Locator considers the user's query, intervention centers on locating the right source and not on the subjective complexities of the user's problem. Mediation at Level 2 is solidly source-oriented and the process of the user is not considered. Locator type of intervention is effective in the later stages in the search process when a specific question can be articulated and a single source located relating to some particular aspect of a focused topic, but the Locator is of limited value when there is vagueness, ambiguity, or uncertainty.

**Level 3: Identifier**

The Identifier, Level 3, expects to see the user only once during the information-seeking process. This hypothetical user has a topic to investigate or a problem to solve more extensive than the single reference question. A group of sources are identified as related to the topic or problem. These are recommended as a group in no particular order, provided in no specific sequence. A request is made and a group of sources is identified. The sources may be from a variety of formats and depths. Typically, when the user comes to the collection with a general topic, seeking information from a number of sources, one comprehensive search is conducted and a "pile" of information is identified as relevant to the general topic without consideration for the users' particular point of view, level of knowledge, or stage in the process. The information is identified usually without any advice on approach or any suggestion of continuing dialogue with the mediator.

The underlying assumption in this level of mediation is the systems point of view and is firmly within the bibliographic paradigm. The system does much to answer questions, but little to accommodate the user's information need. Users' problems are addressed in the collection by identifying the sources that match the topic. Information needs are met by identifying the sources that relate to the general topic under investigation. Users are assumed to approach topics from a uniform perspective, knowledge state, and stage of process. The Identifier level addresses all users in the same way, "tell me your topic or problem and I will help identify the sources that relate to the topic."

Identifiers mediate most effectively when a topic or problem is focused and information is being collected to define the focus. In the early more exploratory stages, Identifiers often overwhelm users with sources and overload them with information. There is a compulsion to name every source that the user might need. That completeness is necessary because there is only one point of contact with the user. Library instruction often falls into this trap. Sessions are planned to identify every possible source, once and for all, so that the user can proceed independently. The process of learning from information access and use is not accommodated well at this level of mediation.

Identifiers do not address the complexity of the learning process that users commonly experience in extended searches. They often mislead users into thinking information seeking is merely identifying sources and not interpreting them. Users tend to think that they are the only ones experiencing confusion because the certainty of the system is predominant in the Identifier's approach. Users are also misled into thinking that the search process does not require exploring and formulating or that the mere collection of sources on the general topic is sufficient for understanding and presenting. Unfortunately, many users encounter severe "writing blocks" when they attempt to prepare to present information gathered in this way.

They have not formed any constructs during the search process and have not reconstrued meaning from the information encountered as the search progressed. A pile of sources do not necessarily lead to understanding and learning.

**Level 4: Advisor**

Level 4, Advisor, is a pattern approach to intervention. The Advisor guides users through a sequence of sources on a particular topic or problem. The Advisor responds to the users who indicate that they have a problem that they intend to investigate in some depth over a period of time. The Advisor not only identifies sources on a topic but also recommends a sequence for using the sources, usually from general to specific. The user asks a complex question or requests information on a topic, and the Advisor recommends a way of navigating through the information by using source *a,* then source *b,* then source *c,* and so on. The Advisor may suggest that the user return periodically during the search or, once the sequence has been recommended, may leave the user to follow the path independently.

The underlying assumption of the Advisor is source-oriented and falls well within the bibliographic paradigm. The user's problem is considered, but within the frame of reference of sources and within a prescribed sequence of use. Therein lies the limitation of the Advisor's mediation. Heavy emphasis is placed on the sources of information, the tools to access the sources, and the appropriate sequence for use of sources. One sequence is recommended for all. The underlying assumption of the Advisor level of mediation is that there is one sequence to use sources to address any topic for every user. Users' problems are expected to be static with a specific end in sight. The underlying assumption is similar to those of "pathfinders," which are standardized descriptions of a generic search offered to those who have a similar topic to investigate.

Although Advisors move along the continuum of mediation to accommodate user's information-seeking process, the individuals creative learning process is not taken into account. No mention is made of the users state of knowledge or stage in the process. The user's dynamic problem, as that person learns from information access and use, and his or her unique individual process are not addressed. Users are easily misled into thinking that there is one right search for all, no matter what their constructs as they enter the process and no matter what ideas they encountered along the way.

## Level 5: Counselor

Level 5, the Counselor, provides intervention into the process of the user. While the concept of information counselor (Debons, 1975; Dosa, 1978) is not new, the role of the Counselor should be expanded to include the recent research into the users' perspective of the search process. Dosa (1978) describes information counselling as

> the interactive process by which an information intermediary (a) assesses the needs and constraints of an individual through in-depth interviewing; (b) determines the optimal ways available to meet such needs; (c) actively assists the client in finding, using, and if needed, applying information; (d) assures systematic follow-up to ascertain that the assistance enabled clients to achieve their goals; (e) develop systematic quality control and evaluation processes. (p. 16)

The underlying assumption is that the user is learning from information in a constructive process as the information search proceeds. There is no one right answer and no fixed sequence for all. The person's problem determines the intervention. The holistic experience is understood, acknowledged, and articulated as an important aspect of mediation. The user and the mediator enter into a dialogue.

The uncertainty principle underlies the Counselor's intervention. Information seeking is viewed as a process of construction rather than a quest for true answers. The user is guided through the dynamic and fluid process of seeking meaning. The recommended sequence of sources of information emerges as the topic or problem evolves in a highly individual way. The information is understood from the frame of reference of the users past experience and the constructs they hold. There are many meanings and many focuses within a general topic. The user forms a focus that is a personal perspective of the general topic under investigation. The Counselor approaches information seeking as a creative, individual process that is dynamic and unique for each person.

In contrast, mediation in Levels 1–4 are based on the principle of certainty. The collection is organized for accurate retrieval. Conflict occurs when the mediator proposes a definite answer, but the user seeks to learn more about a vague topic or an unfocused problem. Mediation within the bibliographic paradigm may be appropriate for the collection stage or when a problem is clearly defined. But when a person is in an exploration stage seeking to formulate a focus, mediation from the bibliographic paradigm projecting a certain system is not likely to match his or her information need.

The Counselor establishes a dialogue that leads to an exploration of strategy and to a sequence for learning. The mediator expects the user to return periodically to reestablish the dialogue based on his or her emerging constructs. The user and the Counselor redefine the problem, determine a strategy, identify additional sources, and a sequence for use. A variety of searches may be conducted with different purposes that match the user's experience at the different points in the process. Strategies change during the process to meet the users' tasks at a particular stage. Sources are recommended in terms of the user's state of knowledge and constructs built from past experience. The relevancy of sources is expected to change during the information search. The entire search process is considered highly individual, creative, and personal. There is no one perfect solution, but there are many approaches in response to the creative formulation of each individual.

The sequence of sources is matched to the stage of the process that the person experiences. The type of search conducted may be an exploratory search for the early stages before formulation or a comprehensive search for the later stages. A range of strategies appropriate to the stage of the process is recommended. Recent studies suggest innovative intervention strategies, such as idea tactics (Bates, 1979), neutral questioning (Dervin and Dewdney, 1986), and activities, including chaining, differentiating, and extracting (Ellis, 1989). Strategies include browsing, skimming and scanning, reflecting, listing ideas, discussing possible choices, and writing short explanations, while tolerating uncertainty.

Four strategies for seeking meaning are to recall, to summarize, to paraphrase, and to extend (Kuhlthau, 1981). Recall is to reflect on what is remembered; summarize is to describe in a capsulized form; paraphrase is to retell in your own words; and extend is to relate to other things or to go beyond the information given. These are basic abilities for using information and activities of learning.

The Counselor is challenged to provide a new kind of mediation that has emerged in the technological information age. A vast increase in the amount of information calls for mediation into the process of information seeking leading to understanding. When an individual seeks meaning, the object is to understand in order to present or to solve a problem. An individual may not need to access all information related to a topic, but only that which pertains to the particular focus he or she has formulated. A focused approach requires more reflection and learning during information seeking. The Counselor guides and supports the user, and offers encouragement, strategies, sources, sequence, and redefinition through exploration and formulation in preparation for collection and resolution.

## LEVELS OF EDUCATION

Instruction, another form of intervention well established in library and information services, may similarly be differentiated into the five levels: Level 1, the Organizer; Level 2, the Lecturer; Level 3, the Instructor; Level 4, the Tutor; and Level 5, the Counselor. Like the Levels of Mediation, the Levels of Education are determined by the complexity of the user's problem, but are differentiated by the number of sessions of instruction rather than the number of sources of information. In this way, education is categorized as being planned for one session, a variety of unconnected sessions, a sequence of related sessions, or holistic interaction over time.

The term *education,* implying the development of transferable knowledge and capabilities, is used rather than instruction, which refers to more immediate outcomes. Terms currently applied to organized teaching, such as bibliographic instruction, library instruction, and information skills instruction, are used interchangeably when referring to current practice across types of libraries. Education is applied as a generic term depicting any planned instruction related to the use of sources found in libraries as well as the use of information in a broader context.

Although education takes place in all types of libraries, it is given priority in those which are part of educational institutions. While this discussion centers on school and academic libraries where instructional sessions are frequently planned for groups of students, much also applies to education, perhaps less formal, given in public and special libraries. The concepts have direct implication and application for education in all types of libraries.

An important consideration for education programs is whether instruction is integrated into the user's problem-solving situation. Much has been written about integrating library instruction with the curriculum of the school or university. Loertscher's (1982) taxonomy of integration of school library services conceptualizes a hierarchy of involvement and coordination. The user's perspective of the Information Search Process offers a further dimension for defining levels of education. The relationship of instruction to the user's specific problem is defined at each level as well as the integration of instruction with the user's information-seeking process. Education below Level 3 is intended for general orientation and is not directed to a specific information need or problem. Levels 3 through 5 are based on the users' information problem. While Levels 3 and 4 *may* be integrated with assignments from the subject areas of the curriculum, Level 5 *must* be integrated with the curriculum and educational objectives of the institution.

In the following description of each of the five levels, the primary objectives, content of instruction, and some typical methods are discussed; as well, examples of instruction are given (see Figure 8–2).

**Level 1: Organizer**

At Level 1, the Organizer gives no instruction. The responsibility of the Organizer is to provide an organized collection of resources with access through a system of classification. The library or information system is considered as a self-service operation in which users are left to their own devices to learn how to locate and use materials.

Most printed instructions and handouts fall within the Organizer's level of education. These materials are planned for the "typical" user rather than an individual user. No human intervention is involved to respond to either the individual's problem or ability. One example is "point-of-use" materials which are printed instructions at the source location to guide people using the source. Another example is pathfinders, which are handouts, usually in chart format, that depict a series of sources to use for addressing a general topic. No intervention with the individual user is provided to match the

| | Level | Description |
|---|---|---|
| 1 | Organizer | No Instruction<br>self-service search in an organized collection |
| 2 | Lecturer | Orienting Instruction<br>single session;<br>overview of services, policies and location<br>of facility and collection;<br>no specific problem |
| 3 | Instructor | Single-Source Instruction<br>variety of independent sessions;<br>instruction on one type of source to<br>address specific problem |
| 4 | Tutor | Strategy Instruction<br>series of sessions;<br>instruction on sequence of sources to<br>address specific problem |
| 5 | Counselor | Process Instruction<br>holistic interaction over time;<br>instruction on identifying and interpreting<br>information to address evolving problem |

**FIG. 8-2.   Levels of Education**

instruction with a unique aspect of a problem or with individual learning style or ability. Other materials which may fall into this category are workbooks and computer-assisted instruction (CAI). Although these materials have potential for assisting some users, their limitations should be clearly recognized.

The Organizer's role underlies all of the other levels of education. Without an organized collection of resources and information, the individual's pursuit of learning and problem solving is severely hampered. Without other levels of education, however, ignorance may be a significant deterrent to the independent pursuit of learning. Access to information is limited and may actually be inhibited by sole reliance on the Organizer.

The primary goal of library instruction according to an American Library Association (1980) Council policy statement is to develop "independent information retrieval" or what Tuckett and Stoffle (1984) refer to as "self-reliant library users." The underlying principle of traditional instruction is the concept that users can be taught to rely on the Organizer level of intervention. Traditional source-oriented instruction has fallen woefully short of expectations for developing independence in using libraries and information. Library skills have not been found to transfer very well to other libraries, let alone to the broader spectrum of information need. We are only now beginning to understand the complexity of what users need to know to be self-reliant in their library use. The Information Search Process indicates that the process of learning from information access and use needs to be learned along with the sources of information. Self-reliant users have skill in interpretating information and seeking meaning as well as skill in locating sources and seeking information. Self-reliant users also know when to proceed on their own and when to ask for mediation at a level beyond that of the Organizer.

**Level 2: Lecturer**

At Level 2, the Lecturer conducts planned orientation in single sessions for large groups. A typical orientation session takes place at the beginning of the semester for a group of incoming students. Orientation sessions are offered in all types of libraries for the full range of potential library users. While generally planned for groups, orientation sessions may be given to individuals as well.

On the Lecturer Level, one session of instruction is offered with the objective of orienting users to the location of the library and to the resources within it. A floor plan is frequently used to illustrate the location of the collections and services of the library. In addition, an overview of procedures and policies are given. Lecture methods are most common, accompanied by a tour of the facility. Multimedia productions, in the form of videos and slide/tapes, are also commonly used. The tendency to tell everything once and for all is an easy trap for the Lecturer, frequently overwhelming students with an abundance of new and unconnected facts and directions.

The Lecturer Level of education is not related to a specific assignment for immediate use, but rather consists of a general orientation for future use. "Treasure Hunts," consisting of a series of unrelated questions that require users to locate a particular source in order to find a specific answer, are sometimes devised. By not being integrated into a particular information problem, Lecturer sessions tend to be superficial and isolated. They cannot be relied on for a substantial amount of recall and transference beyond awareness of general location and procedure.

Although education at this level serves to orient new users to general location and procedures, the expectation that they will be able to use the library effectively following such sessions is unlikely to be met. Much depends on the background and experience of the individual user. All too often library instruction stops at this level, leaving the person with the feeling that he or she is the only one who does not know how to use the library independently. These sessions should be thought of as a beginning or an introduction for further education on other levels.

## Level 3: Instructor

Level 3, the Instructor, provides instruction on a single source usually related to a specific problem or assignment. A resource is identified as being particularly useful for addressing the user's problem or the problem of a group of users. Instruction in how to locate information using the source or tool is offered preferably at the time when the source is expected to be used. A typical example of a lesson at the Instructor Level is a demonstration of how to use an index, such as *Reader's Guide to Periodical Literature* or *Magazine Index,* to locate articles in journals and current periodicals. An understanding of underlying concepts, such as subject access, is important for transference of learning to other similar tools and sources.

The primary objective of the Instructor is to identify appropriate, relevant sources and to teach about their use at the point when the person is ready to use the information. Teaching at the Instructor Level may consist of a variety of independent sessions, each concentrating on one type of source or technology. To be most effective instruction is given at the time that the source is needed to address a problem, rather than in isolation for some future use. The key to motivation and retention is connecting the instruction to the actual information need of the individual user.

The Instructor connects with the teacher or professor by identifying resources for learning. Some advanced planning is needed to schedule the instructional session, but at this level separate teaching responsibilities rather than team teaching requires a minimum of

joint planning. The Instructor Level is source-oriented and is unlikely to accommodate the process of information seeking.

## Level 4: Tutor

At Level 4, the Tutor provides instruction in a series of sessions in
which advice is given on strategies for locating and using sources to
address a specific problem or assignment. At this level, the primary
objective of education is to teach a sequence for using sources and a
search strategy.

Tutors direct users on a path through the sources. The metaphor
of "navigating" through the literature is commonly applied for
describing a sequence of sources. Knapp's (1966) work on conceptual
frameworks provides the foundation for the search strategy approach. The Knapp program was designed to teach students the
library as a system of pathways; "Whoever would use the system
must know the 'way' to use the system. Knowing the way means
understanding the nature of the total system, knowing where to plug
into it, knowing how to make it work" (p. 130).

Tutors help users to understand the relationship among sources in
the library. At this level, users may be led to networks of sources
outside the library as well as to sources in the larger information
environment.

The process of information seeking may be introduced by Tutors.
However, the full-range of experiences and abilities in the process of
learning from information access and use are not addressed. As in
the Instructor Level, skill in the location and use of sources of
information is the primary emphasis, and the reasoning process that
underlies independent research is not developed.

Tutors plan with teachers and professors well in advance of the
assignment to integrate library instruction into the course at significant points. The teacher provides the subject context and the
learning objective, and the librarian offers the resources to meet the
objective. In addition, the Tutor has specific instructional objectives
related to developing information skills that are to be met within the
series of instructional sessions. Tutors and teachers discuss objectives, and resources, and they plan shared teaching responsibilities.

## Level 5: Counselor

At Level 5, the Counselor provides process instruction comprised of holistic interaction over time. Education involves not only identifying sources and advising a sequence, but also counseling in interpreting information to address an evolving problem. Emphasis is on the process of learning from information access and use. Holistic interaction acknowledges the dynamic interplay of thoughts, actions, and feelings in the information-seeking process. Encouragement and support are an important attribute of education at the Counselor Level. The primary objective is to prepare users for future situations of learning from information access and use through knowledge of and ability in the process of information seeking. Strategies for working through the search process are incorporated with strategies for locating sources of information. At the Counselor Level the two forms of intervention, mediation and education, merge into one interactive service of guidance. In a similar way, Neilsen (1982) recommends that mediation and teaching functions be brought together into a new model of service.

The Counselor's instruction is fully integrated with the user's problem. In school and academic settings, the Counselor is an active participant in the instructional team with teachers, administrators, and curriculum planners. The Counselor is actively involved, not only in the delivery of the instruction but also in all phases of designing instruction, from setting goals and objectives, to designing methods and activities, and establishing the means for evaluation. The Counselor is a partner in the implementation of the educational plan.

Each member of the team plays a unique role. Librarians bring expertise in resources, technology, and the information-seeking process. Teachers provide the subject content and the assignment context. Administrators and coordinators provide three kinds of support: philosophical, organizational, and financial. Philosophical support consists of articulating the rationale for information-based learning, which employs a variety of sources rather than one textbook for instructing students. Organizational support offers the logistics necessary for team planning and instruction, particularly the provision of dedicated time. Financial support, of course, consists of the monies to function at this level, particularly for personnel, collection, technology, and facility.

The Counselor Level of education incorporates learning theory into teaching methodology and is based on individual problem solving. The approach involves using, interpreting, and seeking meaning in information from a inquiry or problem-solving perspective. Tuckett and Stoffle (1984) advise that,

> Since problem solving is a critical component of successful library research, teaching these skills is believed to be fully as important as utilizing conceptual frameworks or learning to use specific reference titles in the creation of self-reliant library users. (p. 61)

Educational programs are moving beyond a library orientation, single source, and simple navigation approach to the use of information for thinking and learning. Irving (1985) states that the main thrust of the new approach has been to consider the cognitive environment of the information user and the total framework for acquiring knowledge. Skills for handling information are essentially the same, irrespective of the age of the user, and educational programs can begin in the earliest years of schooling. "It should be possible to not only develop a range of information-handling skills at the earliest age, but also to discern an inherent need for them among the possible applications during schooling" (Irving, p. 5). From the very earliest school years, children can learn to recall, summarize, paraphrase, and extend library materials, thereby building their comprehension abilities as well as their competence in using information. The necessity of enabling students to learn the process of a search for information access and use as well as the sources of information is being recognized in elementary and secondary school library media programs (Irving, 1985; Stripling and Pitts, 1988; Eisenberg and Berkowitz, 1990). Guiding students through the process involves recognition of the crucial early stages of a search when thoughts are being formulated and counseling students in strategies that allow thoughts to develop through the information located in information sources (Kuhlthau, 1985).

Unfortunately, school and academic libraries, the two main library communities involved in education, have not had a common exchange of ideas through a mutual literature and association affiliation. With the exception of a few efforts to open avenues of communication, such as Library Orientation Exchange (LOEX) and the American Library Association Library Instruction Round Table (LIRT), the educational communities remain separate. To appreciate the emerging theory base, it is essential to recognize that there is a concerted move on many fronts to address the larger issue of what it means to be educated in the information age. When we look to the literature we find that school and academic librarians are grappling with similar problems and are finding similar solutions. Librarians in all types of libraries are moving toward a broader view of library skills and are taking learning theory into consideration in planning more meaningful, lasting learning for all information users. Bibliographic instruction in academic libraries has evolved through three models described by Tuckett and Stoffle (1984): a library tool approach, a conceptual frameworks approach, and a theory-based approach. Library skills instruction in school library media centers has evolved through three similar models: a source approach, a pathfinder approach, and a process approach (Kuhlthau, 1987).

Rather than focusing on the use of a particular library, new approaches to education emphasize the underlying concepts of organization of information and how to access information from systems in general. The Dewey Decimal System and Library of Congress Classification System are used as prototypes for demonstrating the concept of classification. The *Reader's Guide to Periodical Literature* and *Magazine Index* are used as examples of how indexing provides access to journal articles. The card catalog and online catalog are used to demonstrate how a collection may be organized with particular access points, stressing the complexity of subject access.

In addition, the broader view of information education goes beyond location of materials to the interpretation and use of information. It centers on thinking about the ideas in information resources rather than merely locating sources in an organized collection. It emphasizes seeking to shape a topic rather than to answer a specific question. It considers the process as well as the product of a search. It is concerned with seeking meaning and gaining understanding. The broader view of information education enables students to learn how to learn in the library.

In educational institutions classroom and course assignments drive the information education program. Assignments that center on inquiry and problem solving lead to the higher-level thinking skills of analysis, synthesis, and presentation. Research assignments can be structured with particular attention to the earliest stages of the Information Search Process. Opportunities need to be provided for students to understand the search process by reflecting on their own efforts and learning ways that their process might be effective in future information use.

The Counselor Level of education encompasses the thoughts, feelings, and actions involved in using information. Counselors are attuned to users' problems and experiences in searching for information. Counselors seek ways to enable people to explore new ideas rather than continuing pedagogical methods that may actually inhibit thinking. Instead of overwhelming the person with mechanics and details at the beginning of a search, the Counselor offers strategies for developing constructs through the information encountered. Counselors accommodate many different learning styles by suggesting a variety of approaches to gathering information, while encouraging the pursuit of individual interest. Counselors enable users to recognize their need for intervention in information seeking and to request a level of mediation appropriate to meet that need.

Preparing students for living and working in an information society is the formidable challenge facing the entire education community from preschool to higher education. The emerging theoretical base for information education — combining learning theory, research in information-seeking behavior, and a broader view of library and information skills — provides a framework for assessing existing instruction and developing new levels of education. Theory-based education prepares students for learning in an information age. The objective of education at the Counselor Level goes beyond obtaining skills for self-reliant library users to achieve an ability for lifelong learning, or what is being called information literacy. Education that guides students through stages of information need, to solve a problem or to shape a topic, enables them to use information for learning. Information literate users are prepared to apply library and information skills through the course of life.

# Chapter 9

## Intervention into the Process of Information Seeking

At the heart of designing process-oriented library and information services is the concept that mediation and education occur on various levels. At the organizer level, the user gathers information from an organized collection independent of direct intervention. The locator/lecturer, identifier/instructor, and advisor/tutor, at levels 2, 3, and 4, increasingly intervene with sources. The counselor, at level 5, becomes involved in the user's interpretation of information for learning and problem solving.

Identifying when intervention is needed and determining what mediation and education are appropriate is the professional's art, or the role of the reflective practitioner. Intervention into the areas where the individual is self sufficient is not only unnecessary but also intrusive and annoying. Mediation into areas where individuals cannot proceed on their own, or can advance only with great difficulty, is enabling and enriching. The area where a person can do with assistance what he or she cannot do alone is the zone of intervention.

The zone of intervention is a concept analogous to the zone of proximal development which relates to intervening in the learning of others. Vygotsky (1978), a soviet psychologist, whose work in the 1940s has had a profound influence on learning theory, developed the concept of an area or zone in which intervention would be most useful to a learner. The zone of proximal development is the distance between actual developmental level as determined by independent problem solving and the level of potential development as determined through problem solving under adult guidance or in collaboration with more capable peers. (p. 131)

The zone of proximal development provides a compelling analogy for understanding intervention into the constructive process of another person.

It is clear from the research on the search process that the information seeker goes to others for help. When a user confers with a librarian a variety of questions about the potential for intervention into the search process arise. How do formal mediators become involved in the constructive process of another person? What is the role and function of intervention? Can the way that other professionals diagnose for intervention be helpful? Schön's (1983) work on "reflection in practice" offers insight into how professionals diagnose and design intervention for an individual's situation. The novice practitioner depends on specific rules and procedures, but the expert relies on experience and theory. Each of the recognized professions have developed rules, procedures, and theories for intervention. The physicians' model of intervention is an example of a way of determining levels of treatment that may be analogized to library and information services mediation.

## PHYSICIANS' ZONE OF TREATMENT

The physician needs to diagnose patients' problems and to determine a course of action for treating. The interaction patterns of diagnostic practice has been studied extensively (Ruben, 1990). Analysis of the communication and interaction between the physician and patient reveals a pattern that may be useful for defining the zone of intervention for mediating in information seeking (Mokros, 1990). The physician/patient interaction has been characterized as occurring in five zones of treatment (see Figure 9–1). In the first zone (Z1), the problem is self-diagnosed and treatment is self-administered. The patient notices problematic symptoms, diagnoses the problem without consulting a physician, and administers treatment.

In each of the other zones (Z2–Z5) the patient consults the

| | |
|---|---|
| Z1 | Problem self-diagnosed |
| | Treatment self-administered |
| Z2–Z5 | Problem diagnosed through interview |
| | a. Problem statement |
| | b. Background—Patient's history |
| | c. Diagnosis using theory base Physical or Psychological |
| | d. Treatment prescribed |

Physical
Z2 Medication
Z3 Medications
Z4 Series of treatments

Psychological

Z5

a. Dialogue
b. Transference
c. Internalization
d. Construction
e. Change

**FIG. 9–1.  Physicians' Zone of Treatment**

physician and the physician prescribes the treatment. In an initial interview the physician elicits a problem statement, a description of symptoms, and a history, an explanation of related background information. The first 5 to 10 minutes of the interview are critical for gathering information to diagnose the zone of treatment for the patient. Based on professional theory, the physician makes a diagnosis as to whether the problem is physical or psychological. Physical problems are then diagnosed as falling into a particular zone of treatment (Z2–Z4). Those problems falling within the second zone of treatment (Z2) are treated with a single medication or prescription. Patients diagnosed as requiring the third zone of treatment (Z3) are given several different medications. Problems falling within the fourth zone of treatment (Z4) require a series of treatments that may include a combination of medications and surgery.

When the patient's problem is diagnosed as a psychological or a "head" problem, the fifth zone of treatment (Z5) is prescribed. The physician enters into a dialogue with the patient that is expected to extend over a period of time. The fifth zone encompasses manipulation of the problem through transference and internalization, with construction and change as an anticipated outcome.

The zone of treatment may be thought of as a continuum with the person's problem determining the entrance and exit points. The solution to the problem, in this case when the patient is cured, signals end of treatment. A problem may begin at Z1 and be addressed in each successive zone or may be diagnosed at any point as needing treatment in Z2–Z5. Professional judgment is crucial to the patients welfare as overtreating a problem may be as hazardous as undertreating.

## ZONE OF INTERVENTION BASED ON PHYSICIANS' ZONE OF TREATMENT

The zone of intervention for mediation and education into the Information Search Process may be charted using the zone of treatment as an analogy for identifying patterns in professional/client interaction (see Figure 9–2). Five zones of intervention, which parallel those depicted in the illustration of the physicians' approach to diagnosing a patient's problem, have been identified.

In the first zone (Z1), the problem is self-diagnosed, the need for information self-determined, and a search self-conducted. In each of the other zones (Z2–Z5), the person consults the librarian who diagnoses the zone of intervention from a query or a problem

---

Z1
    Problem self-diagnosed
    Search self-conducted
Z2-Z5
    Problem diagnosed through interview
    a. Problem statement or request
    b. Background — task, interest, time, availability
    c. Diagnosis using theory base: Product or Process
    d. Intervention negotiated

Product
Z2 Right source
Z3 Relevant sources
Z4 Sequence of sources

Process
Z5
a. Dialogue
b. Exploration
c. Formulation
d. Construction
e. Learning
f. Application

**FIG. 9–2.  Zone of Intervention**

statement. Through an interview the background of the problem is elicited. That background information centers on four criteria that were found in the studies of the search process. These criteria can be used for making elaborative choices: the requirements of the task, the personal interest of the user, the time allotted for completion, and the availability of information.

Intervention is negotiated between the user and the librarian, rather than prescribed as in the case of the physician. The first few minutes of the interview are crucial for determining the zone of intervention. Based on professional experience and theory, the librarian makes a diagnosis as to whether the problem is a product (source) problem or process problem. Product problems, those which can be solved by specific sources, are then diagnosed as falling into a particular Zone of Intervention from 2 through 4 (Z2–Z4). Those queries falling within the second zone of intervention (Z2) are offered the right source. Users' problems diagnosed as requiring the third zone of intervention (Z3) are led to or given a group of relevant sources. Users' whose problems fall within the fourth zone of intervention (Z4) are offered a group of relevant sources and a recommended sequence for use. Interventions in Z2–Z4 are source- or product-oriented and address problems that are expected to remain static.

When the user's problem is diagnosed as changing and fluid the fifth zone of intervention (Z5) is necessary, the application of a process approach to mediation and education. The librarian enters into a dialogue with the user and the interaction extends over a period of time. The fifth zone of intervention (Z5) encompasses exploration and formulation for construction and learning in the Information Search Process. The anticipated outcome of the intervention is application of the user's new construction to the problem at hand. In addition, increased self-awareness of the search process may be expected to be learned and applied to other new situations of information seeking.

The zone of intervention may be thought of as a continuum, similar to the zone of treatment, with the state of the user's problem determining the entrance and exit points. The solution to the problem signals the end of intervention. A problem may be diagnosed as falling into any of the five zones of intervention. As in the case of the physician and patient, however, professional judgment is crucial to avoid either overintervening or underintervening in a problem.

## LEVELS OF MEDIATION FOR THE ZONES OF INTERVENTION

The levels of mediation, described in Chapter 8, parallel the five zones of intervention. The Organizer would match the first zone (Z1), which requires an organized collection but no direct intervention. The Locator/ Lecturer would match the second zone (Z2) by offering ready reference or orientation intervention. The Identifier/Instructor provides standard reference intervention in the third zone (Z3). The Advisor/ Tutor would offer pattern intervention or a sequence of instructional sessions in the fourth zone (Z4). The Counselor would engage in process intervention in the fifth zone (Z5).

The model of the Information Search Process and the uncertainty principle are proposed as a frame of reference for matching the level of mediation and education to the user's zone of intervention. The information professional assesses the user's problem, determines what role best fits the user's need for intervention, and designs mediation and education to match the user's need for intervention. The user's need for sources and information are incorporated with the user's need for process intervention. The level of mediation and education may be used as a basis for designing services that are directly responsive to the stage of the user's problem in a process of information seeking.

The Counselor level is emerging and developing in response to the demands of the information environment. The changing information environment has prompted a reassessment of traditional library and information services and requires information professionals to assume new roles to support users.

## INTERVENTION IN AN INFORMATION ENVIRONMENT

Intervention in information seeking is profoundly influenced by the total information environment. Wilson (1977) states that everyone has set habits or routines for keeping his or her internal model of the world up to date. An examination of common information habits and routines reveals some basic problems inherent in the information age. It is becoming increasingly apparent that far too many people are information poor in an information rich environment. How do individual habits and routines intersect with the organized collection of information?

The concept of information need is central to library and information service. However, information need is commonly viewed from the system's perspective rather than the user's viewpoint. Traditionally, information need is defined as a gap in knowledge or a lack of a specific piece of information. Within the course of daily living, people rarely experience "an information need" as depicted by the information system. People have questions that need answers and problems that need solving, but rarely are these translated into an information need to be addressed in an organized collection. The questions and problems people do bring to the information system are likely to be the easiest for the system to address. For the most part questions and problems fall into two levels of mediation, the Locator for ready reference and the Identifier for collecting and gathering in the later stages of the search process. When librarians confine their intervention to questions, problems, and concerns that can be readily articulated by the user, the opportunity may be lost for opening up the library to those who have an initial, vague interest or a sense of wanting to know more. The concept of information need may require expansion to include vague notions, hunches, and hints of interest. Intervention to address an urge to know, the will to learn, and the desire to understand is considerably more difficult to provide. The concept of a zone of intervention indicates an intervention need in addition to an information need to be accommodated by the mediator.

Wilson's (1977) discussion of interests and concerns raises a difficult distinction related to mediation in an information rich environment. He recommends that mediation concentrate on concerns that lead to action rather than less compelling interests of users. The process of information seeking, however, may not be so readily divided between interests and concerns. Interest and concerns may be experienced in a continuum rather than two disparate approaches to information need. Within the context the Information Search Process, a general vague notion of an area of interest may gradually become a personalized concern in a series of stages. A person becomes more intellectually engaged as a personal view is formed through reading and reflecting on the information encoun-

tered in the process of the search. Concerns originate and grow out
of vague interests. User's interests should not be taken lightly and
need to be considered as part of the exploratory stage of an extended
search process. In the series of studies described in Chapters 3
through 5, the participants began with some interest in general topics
but their interest increased during the search as their thoughts
became clearer and more focused. One person's experience serves to
illustrate the point. Starting with a high school interest in the general
topic on the issue of capital punishment, that student had developed
a high degree of personal involvement in the problem by the time the
project was completed. Upon later reflection, the paper was referred
to as, "my work of art," which should be published rather than left
"in a drawer not doing anything." Initial interest for this young
person had become a genuine concern which had continued through
college, through further studies in law and finally into the practice of
law. Interests may be concerns at an earlier stage in the process. A
concern may be a focus at the middle of the process on which to base
judgments of what relevant information is pertinent to resolution of
the particular problem.

   The concept of a constructive process underlying information use
is the principle for library and information services for the information age. The uncertainty principle addresses the complexity of the
process of learning from information access and use, the connection
between interests and concerns, and the role of mediation and
education for increased access and enhanced use.


## OLD METAPHORS AND NEW MEANINGS

Some underlying principles and assumptions upon which library and
information services have been based are shifting to accommodate the
new information environment. Many metaphors are holdovers from
a former era, established in the industrial age of more simple technologies, and firmly grounded in the bibliographic paradigm. New
metaphors that envision the way we use information in an information
rich technological society are emerging. Considerable conflict arises
when an old metaphor is applied in a shifting paradigm.

   Our concepts of knowing and learning have changed in the
information age. Consideration for the limitations on human cogni-

tive ability as well as appreciation for the flexibility and uniqueness of human thinking becomes an important element in information provision. The rate of human cognition is limited in the amount of information that can be processed at a given time, as Miller's formula of the magic 7 succinctly summarizes. On the one hand, humans need time for reflection and accommodation for self-pacing. On the other hand, humans are capable of great diversity in thinking and individuality in construction, as those involved in artificial intelligence and expert systems have come to appreciate. Individual focus and formulation become essential in the information environment. A focus provides a personal perspective on which to build an information search. Selective attention, for which human beings are uniquely suited, is the basis of judgments of relevance which are individual, personal, and hard to predict from person to person.

## Card Catalog

The card catalog as a metaphor for access to information matched the bibliographic paradigm. The card catalog metaphor portrays the complete organized collection indexed on 3 by 5 cards, arranged alphabetically and assigned a designated code to respond to a specific request for a source by title, author, or subject. The underlying premise is that of a certain system fostering a right source approach to information provision. The card catalog metaphor promotes self-service gathering for completion rather than mediated exploration for formulation. The card catalog metaphor fosters the one generic search for location of sources rather than an individualized search for use and construction. The card catalog metaphor suggests static topics rather than dynamic problems. A new metaphor would encompass the process of learning from information proceeding from uncertainty to understanding. Perhaps a hypermedia metaphor might match the present age with its capacity for tailoring responses to an individual's need to know.

The problem of the uncertain person encountering the certain system may be compounded rather than eased by current use of technology in automated systems. For example, online public access catalogs may increase the perception of certainty but limit exploration and formulation. Access in general may be thought to be enhanced whereas access for personal construction actually may be inhibited. Access to information which leads to learning and finding meaning calls for process intervention. The uncertainty principle indicates that individuals need to tolerate their own uncertainty in order to learn. Uncertainty is not only accepted but also expected. In addition, the mediator needs to tolerate uncertainty as well and to develop intervention that goes beyond toleration to accommodation.

## Steps for Research Papers

A metaphor related to library instruction that no longer works for us is the traditional steps for doing research papers, which were regarded by many as the way to do library research. The traditional model recommends that students follow these steps when preparing for a research paper or term paper (Warriner and Griffith, 1973):

Step 1 — Select and limit the subject

Step 2 — Prepare a working bibliography

Step 3 — Prepare a preliminary outline

Step 4 — Read and take notes

Step 5 — Assemble notes and write final outline

Step 6 — Write first Draft

Step 7 — Write revised final draft with footnotes and bibliography.

This model is misleading to students. This oversimplification recommends that students proceed directly from selecting and limiting the subject to preparing a working bibliography and preliminary outline, neglecting the thinking and formulation that is necessary during the search for information, particularly in the early stages. Reading about the topic is listed after the topic is well defined in an outline. Selecting and limiting are depicted as taking place before any materials are gathered or read, implying that a subject can be narrowed from what a person knows rather than from what he or she learns from sources. All mention of the complex, creative process of formulating thoughts about a topic from the information encountered in the search in preparation for writing is omitted. There is, however, no research to support this widely used pedagogical advice. These steps may have been tolerable in the industrial age when there was a limited, manageable amount of information available to the average person, but they are not suitable in the information age. In the former age the research paper was primarily an academic exercise. Today the need for and use of information is central to our way of working and learning throughout our lives. The Information Search Process represents the process of learning from information enabling people to cope with overload in an information rich environment.

## Concept of Enough

Another example of changing meanings is the concept of "enough." What is "enough" was a relatively simple notion when a person could gather all there was to know on a topic. The concept of "enough" is quite a different matter in the present-day information environment. Understanding what is "enough" is essential for making sense of the information around us. "Enough" relates to seeking meaning in a quantity of information by determining what one needs to know and by formulating a perspective on which to build. The Information Search Process treats the concept of "enough" as what is "enough" to make sense for oneself. The concept of "enough" is applied to the tasks in each stage of the process. There must be the ability to recognize an information need, to explore information on a general topic, to formulate a specific focus, to gather information pertaining to the specific focus, to prepare to share what has been learned, or to solve a problem.

## Concept of Privacy

Many other traditional meanings and principles are being redefined within the information age. For example, the privacy principle as commonly practiced may raise barriers to constructive access. Overzealous protection of the privacy of the user, in some instances, may impede the process of learning from information access and use. The question of why a person wants to know is commonly considered beyond the boundaries of privacy. Excessive concern with privacy, however, may limit the development of higher levels of intervention. Users may misinterpret limited questioning by librarians as a lack of interest in them and their inquiry. Professional perspective needs to balance users' need to pursue interests with a sensitive concerns for their right to privacy.

The debate over the intrusive question may cloud the real issue at the heart of the matter, that of meeting the user's need for intervention as well as the user's need for information. Findings of the studies of users' perspective of information seeking suggest an approach to intervention that might protect users' privacy while assisting them in their search process. Participants explained that in a search for information they were seeking to find a story. Dialogue between the Counselor and the user may center on discovering the story. The notion that there are multiple meanings in information is essential for eliciting users' stories and constructions as they emerge in the process of information seeking. The professional mediator enters a dialogue with the user by taking hunches and vague utterances seriously, offering encouragement, and eliciting personal perspective by replacing the intrusive "Why do you want to know?" with a suggestive "Tell me more."

In an information environment, both users and mediators need to better understand the tasks of information seeking. Old metaphors project collection tasks that center solely on gathering and completing. New metaphors for exploration and formulation are called for to characterize the full range of complex tasks within the stages of the Information Search Process.

## PROCESS-ORIENTED LIBRARY AND INFORMATION SERVICES

Library and information services comprise two basic forms of intervention with users: Reference and instruction, which have been redefined as mediation and education. The Information Search Process and the uncertainty principle have implications for diagnosing the users' zone of intervention in each of these services.

Traditionally, reference services have been based on sources rather than process. Heavy emphasis on locating the right source and the goal of accuracy detract attention from the more dynamic aspects of information seeking. Mediation into the Information Search Process requires expanding the more traditional roles of the librarian from Locator, Identifier, and Advisor for accessing sources to Counselor for learning and problem solving. Awareness of the process in which the user is learning from information access and use by exploring and formulating during a search broadens the mediators' scope from concentration on sources to consideration of use. The zone of intervention varies according to the users' task and state of knowledge.

In a similar way instruction has been based on learning the sources in an organized collection rather than on understanding the process of learning from information access and use. The very term, bibliographic instruction connotes teaching sources without attention to use, interpretation, or meaning. Problems with transference of skills have been recognized as pervasive and have been widely critized. By centering exclusively on the sources and the product of a search, the dynamic process of using information has been neglected. Process strategies for exploring and formulating enable students to learn how to learn. Educational programs that offer users' an understanding of their search task are better aligned with the natural progression of their thoughts and feelings. Education programs that teach students to become aware of their own process of learning from information access and use prepare them for the process of using information in other situations of an information need. By identifying the zone of intervention the mediator instructs only in those areas where the user can learn.

Classification systems are based on the prototype of a generic search rather than an individual process of construction. The organizer's task of providing all there is, all of the time, in every instance falls within the traditional approach to library and information system design. Information overload and information anxiety are problems resulting from this approach. Designers of online catalogs, end-user bibliographic databases, and searcher training programs need to address the question of how the user's process can be accommodated in interfaces between information systems and users. In this way, the system may be made to accommodate the zone of intervention.

The process approach does not advocate throwing out all traditional practices. Rather, it proposes building on existing programs of service to incorporate a sensitivity to process to better meets users' needs in an information rich environment. The mediator, with a clear understanding of the user's zone of intervention within a dynamic process, is armed for expanding and changing common practice.

# Chapter 10

## Process-oriented Library and Information Services

Library and information services are in a critical period of redefinition and change. The traditional bibliographic paradigm, centering on the location of sources, is no longer adequate for accommodating the full range of users' problems in the information age. The traditional approach is limited to the task of locating sources and information but does not take into account the tasks of interpreting, formulating, and learning in the process of information seeking. Increased access to vast amounts of information requires services that center on seeking meaning rather than merely on locating sources. In an earlier industrial age, the bibliographic approach to services may have been sufficient for addressing users' information needs. Advances in technology, however, have shifted the task of information seeking from locating to sense making. Services must be redefined to respond to the new fundamental task of information users.

When the user's process of learning from information access and use is recognized as an important element in information provision, we become aware of a critical gap in the theoretical foundations of library and information science. Theory for explaining users' experience in the process of seeking meaning from information is tentative and speculative, and is in need of a more extensive research base. A survey of the literature of the field reveals an underlying problem of overemphasis on product and underemphasis on process.

The user's holistic experience in information seeking is not being addressed. Traditional emphasis on sources has detracted from the process of constructing meaning from information within sources. Users' problems center not only on locating sources of information but also on seeking meaning from sources. Seeking meaning incorporates an individual's cognitive, physical, and affective experience. Library and information services that stop short of intervention into the meaning-making process fail to meet users' information needs in the information age.

Theory enables us to rise above the confusion of everyday life to see patterns, to understand principles, and to act purposefully and productively. In order to provide library and information services that purposefully and productively respond to a range of users' information problems, we need a theoretical framework with patterns and principles on which to build. Since theory in library and information science is presently inadequate for fully explaining the process of learning from information access and use, we have looked to the principles of learning in general for a borrowed theoretical explanation. A generic explanation of learning as a process of construction provided a conceptual premise for studying users' experience in information-seeking situations.

The theoretical premise that explains learning as a process of construction led to the conceptual assumption that information seeking is a process of construction. This conceptual assumption derived from the borrowed theory was examined in a series of empirical studies of people in actual situations of information seeking. Five studies were conducted; in the beginning, qualitative methods were used to investigate the assumption and derive a hypothesis. Next, longitudinal and quantitative methods were used to test and verify the initial findings. In this way the borrowed theory was redefined into a grounded theory for library and information services.

## PATTERNS IN THE INFORMATION SEARCH PROCESS

The series of studies revealed common patterns in users' experience in the process of seeking meaning from information. Users experienced the process of information seeking as a series of thoughts, feelings, and actions. Thoughts which began as uncertain, vague, and ambiguous became clearer, more focused, and specific as the process progressed. Feelings of anxiety and doubt became more confident and certain. Through their actions, students sought information relevant to the general topic at the beginning and pertinent to the focused topic toward closure. A task for each stage was identified; so too were strategies for accomplishing the task and the mood or attitude most productive for the user to assume at that point in the process. Formulation of a focus or a personal perspective of the topic or problem was a pivotal point in the search process. At this point, feelings shifted from anxious to more confident, thoughts changed from uncertain to more clear, and interest increased.

Patterns in experience were articulated in a model of the search process describing typical tasks, thoughts, feelings, actions, strategies, and moods within six stages: Initiation, Selection, Exploration, Formulation, Collection, and Presentation. The model was verified in longitudinal studies as well as in large-scale studies of diverse samples of library users.

At "Initiation," when a person first becomes aware of a lack of knowledge or understanding, feelings of uncertainty and apprehension are common. At this point, the task is merely to recognize a need for information. Thoughts center on contemplating the problem, comprehending the task, and relating the problem to prior experience and knowledge. Actions frequently involve discussing possible topics and approaches.

During "Selection," the task is to identify and select the general topic to be investigated or the approach to be pursued. Feelings of uncertainty often give way to optimism after the selection has been made, and there is a readiness to begin the search. Thoughts center on weighing perspective topics against the criteria of personal interest, assignment requirements, information available, and time allotted. The outcome of each possible choice is predicted, and the topic or approach judged to have the greatest potential for success is selected. Typical actions are to confer with others. Some may make a preliminary search of information available, and skim and scan for an overview of alternative topics. When, for whatever reason, selection is delayed or postponed, feelings of anxiety are likely to intensify until the choice is made.

"Exploration" is characterized by feelings of confusion, uncertainty, and doubt which frequently increase during this time. The task is to investigate information on the general topic in order to extend personal understanding. Thoughts center on becoming oriented and sufficiently informed about the topic to form a focus or a personal point of view. At this stage, an inability to express precisely what information is needed makes communication between the user and the system awkward. Actions involve locating information about the general topic, reading to become informed, and relating new information to what is already known. Strategies that open opportunities for forming new constructs, such as listing facts that seem particularly pertinent and reflecting on engaging ideas, may be most helpful during this time. Strategies that foster an indicative rather than an invitational mood, such as taking detailed notes, may thwart the process by seeking premature closure. Information encountered rarely fits smoothly with previously-held constructs, and information from different sources commonly seems inconsistent and incompatible. Users may find the situation quite discouraging and threatening, causing a sense of personal inadequacy as well as frustration with the system. Some people actually may be inclined to abandon the search altogether at this stage.

"Formulation" is the turning point of the search process when feelings of uncertainty diminish and confidence increases. The task is to form a focus from the information encountered. Thoughts involve identifying and selecting ideas and forming a focused perspective of the topic. A focus in the search process is comparable to a hypothesis in the process of construction. The topic becomes more personalized at this stage if construction is taking place. While a focus may be formed in a sudden moment of insight, it is more likely to emerge gradually as constructs become clearer. During this time, a change in feelings is commonly noted, with indications of increased confidence and a sense of clarity.

"Collection" is the stage in the process when interaction between the user and the information system functions most effectively and efficiently. At this point, the task is to gather information related to the focused topic. Thoughts center on defining, extending, and supporting the focus. Actions involve selecting information relevant to the focused perspective of the topic and making detailed notes on that which pertains specifically to the focus. General information on the topic is no longer relevant after formulation. The user, with a clearer sense of direction, can specify the need for relevant, focused information to mediators and to systems, thereby facilitating a comprehensive search of all available resources. Feelings of confidence continue to increase as uncertainty subsides with interest in the project deepening.

In "Presentation," feelings of relief are common with a sense of satisfaction if the search has gone well or disappointment if it has not. The task is to complete the search and to prepare to present or otherwise use the findings. Thoughts concentrate on culminating the search with a personalized synthesis of the topic or problem. Actions involve a summary search in which decreasing relevance and increasing redundancy are noted in the information encountered. Organizing strategies, such as outlining, for preparing to present or otherwise use the information are applied.

## UNDERLYING THEORETICAL PRINCIPLE FOR SERVICES

The next element in theory building is to state findings and patterns revealed through rigorous research as a theoretical principle. A theoretical premise is proposed for library and information services in the form of an uncertainty principle.

Uncertainty, the predominant experience in the early stages of the search process, is not being sufficiently addressed in library and information services. The uncertainty principle states that uncertainty is a cognitive state which commonly causes affective symptoms of anxiety and lack of confidence. Uncertainty and anxiety can be expected in the early stages of the Information Search Process. The affective symptoms of uncertainty, confusion, and frustration are associated with vague, unclear thoughts about a topic or question. As knowledge states shift to more clearly focused thoughts, a parallel shift occurs in feelings of increased confidence. Uncertainty due to a lack of understanding, a gap in meaning, or a limited construct initiates the process of information seeking.

The uncertainty principle is expanded by six corollaries, each of which offers an explanation of a particular aspect of the Information Search Process. The six corollaries are: process corollary, formulation corollary, redundancy corollary, mood corollary, prediction corollary, and interest corollary.

## Process Corollary

The process of information seeking involves construction in which the user actively pursues understanding and meaning from the information encountered over a period of time. The process is commonly experienced in a series of thoughts and feelings that shift from vague and anxious to clear and confident as the search progresses.

## Formulation Corollary

Formulation is thinking, developing an understanding, and extending and defining a topic from the information encountered in a search. The formulation of a focus or a guiding idea is a critical, pivotal point in a search when a general topic becomes clearer and a particular perspective is formed as the user moves out of uncertainty to understanding.

## Redundancy Corollary

The interplay of seeking what is expected or redundant, and encountering what is unexpected or unique, results in an underlying tension within the search process. Redundant information fits into what we already know and is promptly recognized as being relevant or irrelevant. Unique information does not match our constructs and requires reconstruction to be recognized as useful. Redundancy may be expected to increase as uncertainty decreases. The lack of redundancy at the beginning of the search process may be an underlying cause of anxiety related to uncertainty.

## Mood Corollary

Mood, a stance or attitude that the user assumes, opens or closes the range of possibilities in a search. An invitational mood leads to expansive actions, and an indicative mood leads to conclusive actions. The user's mood may shift during the search process. An invitational mood may be more appropriate for the early stages of the search, and an indicative mood more appropriate for the latter stages.

## Prediction Corollary

The search process may be thought of as a series of choices based on predictions of what will happen if a particular action is taken. Predictions are based on expectations derived from constructs built on past experience. Each of us constructs our own unique personal worlds. Therefore, the predictions and choices made in the search process may vary widely from user to user. Predictions may change during the search process as the user moves from uncertainty to understanding.

## Interest Corollary

Interest increases as the exploratory inquiry leads to formulation in the Information Search Process. Motivation and intellectual engagement intensify along with construction. Personal interest may increase as uncertainty decreases.

In the uncertainty principle, the constructivist view is articulated as a theory for information provision. Information seeking is described as a series of stages in a process of construction in which the individual moves from uncertainty to understanding. A process approach to information provision is proposed to accommodate a series of dynamic stages of seeking meaning from information. The uncertainty principle offers information professionals a theoretical basis for diagnosing users' problems to determine appropriate intervention. Different types or levels of intervention are needed for the different stages of the search process.

## LEVELS OF LIBRARY AND INFORMATION SERVICES

The concept of levels of intervention within the two basic services of reference and instruction provides a way of envisioning how the process might be accommodated. Reference services are differentiated in five levels of mediation: organizer, locator, identifier, advisor, and counselor. Instructional services are differentiated in five levels of education: organizer, lecturer, instructor, tutor, and counselor.

At level 1, the organizer provides an organized collection, but no intervention in terms of mediation or education. The organizer level of intervention depends on the user's capacity for conducting a self-service search. At level 2, the locator intervenes with one source in a single encounter. The locator offers ready reference intervention by responding to a single query with an answer in the form of a fact or a source. The lecturer, on level 2, provides instruction in a single session with the purpose of offering an overview of services and sources in a general orientation not related to a specific problem or topic.

At level 3, the identifier mediates by providing a group of sources related to a topic. In this standard reference intervention, a subject search is conducted in response to a problem statement derived from a reference interview. A group or bunch of sources related to the topic are recommended in no particular order. The instructor, on level 3, teaches about sources in one or several independent, single sessions. The purpose of the instruction is to introduce a particular group of sources or type of source, usually to address a specific problem or task.

At level 4, the advisor, provides pattern intervention or a sequence for using sources. In a reference interaction the problem is stated, assistance negotiated, and sequence recommended. The tutor, on level 4, provides instruction on a strategy for navigating through a search. The tutor conducts a series of related sessions instructing on the sequence for using sources to address a particular problem or task.

At level 5, the counselor addresses the holistic experience of seeking meaning within the process of an information search. The counselor provides mediation by disclosing an evolving problem for redefinition through dialogue, and recommending strategies, sources, and sequence for each stage in the search process. Instruction at this level is embedded in the process and educates users to identify and interpret information as a search progresses.

## DIAGNOSING NEED FOR INTERVENTION

The concept of a zone of intervention has been introduced for diagnosing users' need for one of the five levels of mediation and education. The zone of intervention is that area in which a user can do with guidance and assistance what he or she could not do alone. The zone moves him or her along in the Information Search Process. Intervention outside of this zone is intrusive, on the one side, and overwhelming, on the other. Intervention on both sides of the zone of intervention is inefficient and unnecessary. The concept of a zone of intervention is a new approach to analyzing users' information needs and calls for an active diagnostic role for librarians and information professionals. The critical element in diagnosis is whether users' problems create a source or a process information need or some combination of both.

The practitioner applies theory and experience to the professional art of diagnosing users' problems. An analogy is drawn with the physicians' zone of treatment in diagnosing a patient. Five zones of intervention which parallel five zones of treatment of the physician are described. In zone 1, the user's problem is self-diagnosed and the search self-conducted, as the patient's problem is self-diagnosed and the treatment is self-administered. In zones of intervention 2 through 4, the user's problem is diagnosed as requiring product (source) intervention, similar to the physicians' diagnosis of physical or psychological problems. Zone 2 questions may be responded to by a single source or right answer, like the physical problem requiring one medication. Zone 3 problems may be addressed by a group of relevant sources, like the physician's treatment with several appropriate medications. Zone 4 problems may be addressed by recommending a sequence for using relevant sources, similar to the physician's series of treatments. Users' problems within the fifth zone of intervention, however, are recognized as more complex and dynamic, similar to the physician diagnosing a psychological problem. In zone 5, the user's problem or task is recognized as evolving over time in the process of information seeking requiring exploration, formulation, and construction.

Each of the five zones of intervention corresponds to one of the five levels of mediation. Users' problems diagnosed as in zone 1 may be considered within the range of the organizer in level 1, requiring no mediation. Zone 2 questions fall within the range of the locator in level 2, answered by the right source. Zone 3 problems may be addressed by the identifier in level 3, by providing a group of relevant sources. Zone 4 problems are within the range of the advisor in level 4, addressed by recommending a sequence for using relevant sources. Zone 5 problems involve the more ongoing role of the counselor in level 5.

In a similar way the five levels of education correspond to the five zones of intervention. Problems within zone 1 are addressed in a self-conducted search with no instruction. Users with problems within zone 2 are provided orientation by the lecturer. Users with zone 3 problems receive instruction in an isolated session by the instructor. Those with problems in zone 4 are taught strategies by the tutor. At the lower level 1, the organizer, and at the upper level 5, the counselor, mediation and education roles merge into a single approach to library and information service.

Diagnosing users' problems to determine an appropriate level of intervention is a highly reflective activity in which the practitioner relies not only on the patterns and underlying principles of a theoretical framework but also on sound professional experience. In other contexts, Schön (1982) describes the reflective practitioner as one who has internalized the underlying principles of the profession and develops the ability for continued learning and problem solving throughout his or her career. Reflection-in-action is a "thinking on your feet" approach to solving problems frequently observed in the seasoned professional. An overarching theory, combined with an intuitive feel for the situation, guides the reflection-in-action of an experienced professional. In this way, practitioners can recognize and engage that which is shifting and turbulent in their practice.

Reflective information professionals need to redefine library and information services in this shifting and turbulent period. Reflection-in-action, guided by an internalization of the underlying patterns and principles in the process of information seeking, is a way to develop a new approach to services. Developing the role of the counselor in the information search process will require considerable reflection-in-action as well as extensive conversation, experimentation, and documentation among reflective practitioners.

## PROGRAMMATIC IMPLEMENTATION

While the uncertainty principle, levels of mediation and education, and the concept of a zone of intervention have been articulated as a basis for process-oriented practice, there is no neat package of interventions that can be handed to librarians and information specialists. On the contrary, process intervention depends upon the reflective practitioner who understands the dynamic process of learning from information access and use and incorporates that awareness into all aspects of intervening with users. There are three important elements of process-oriented library and information services: (1) identification of the zone of intervention, (2) establishment of dialogue as a strategy, and (3) acknowledgment of stages in the search process.

The identification of the zone of intervention is the first component in responding to users' need for process intervention. Intervention is not needed in every instance, in every search. Identifying those instances when intervention is needed and determining the level of intervention is the basis of process-oriented services. In any library or information system, each of the levels of mediation and education may be considered as common practice. Many people will use the library as a self-service collection. In most instances independent access will remain the primary use of the system. Location will continue to be a critical service for direct, simple questions and orientation will be an important aspect of education. The identifier/instructor and advisor/tutor will continue to serve those people whose problems are extensive and ongoing, but in the collection rather than the exploration stage. The counselor level of intervention, however, needs to be developed within the frame of reference of the Information Search Process and the uncertainty principle. Problems currently being addressed by the locator/lecturer, identifier/instructor, and advisor/tutor may well occur in the zone of intervention better served by a counselor. The ability to identify what users can and cannot do without help is essential for developing process-oriented intervention. The concept of identifying a zone of intervention needs to be incorporated into common library practice.

Establishing dialogue as a strategy is a second step in responding to users who need counseling in the process of information seeking. The need to discuss and talk about the topic and the process is a natural instinct to be brought into mediation practice. The reference interview may be extended to a conversation which offers the user an opportunity to tell a story about the problem. The concept of a narrative or story may be much more appropriate for articulating an information need in the stages prior to formulation than that of a formal query, request, or question. In this way, emphasis is placed on the inquiry instead of the query. The conversation sets the stage for an ongoing dialogue throughout the process. Both the user and the mediator expect continuing interaction rather than a single incident. Dialogue centers on the users' narrative and is directed, to a large extent, by the user, particularly in the early stages. The sources and mechanics of the search, and the presentation and product of the task, are not allowed to overshadow the basic interest and concern of the user. Dialogue as a strategy facilitates formulation as well as promoting more conceptual search techniques. Such interaction offers opportunities for expressing an emerging focus and developing personal perspective. The mediator may share in the user's discovery and learning in the process of the search. The mediator may participate in the intellectual engagement of the user and in the user's increased interest and personal involvement. Professional responsibility deepens along with competence in making a clear distinction between enabling guidance and intrusive interference.

Acknowledgment of stages in the Information Search Process is another essential component of process-oriented intervention. The process model offers a way to conceptualize and articulate the experience of a person involved in an extended search. The mediator clearly understands the process of the user and the sequence of tasks to be undertaken. Expectation of uncertainty, which initiates the inquiry, and tolerance for confusion before formulation provide an invitation for dialogue and the establishment of a range of associated strategies.

Encouragement and support are an integral part of the intervention along with a sequence of recommended sources and strategies for formulating, extending, and defining. Strategies include various forms of writing, charting, discussing, and, where appropriate, use of peer support and team efforts along with more traditional search techniques.

## THE COUNSELOR IN THE INFORMATION SEARCH PROCESS

Within the information environment a greater number of users' problems are within the fifth zone of intervention. Library and information professionals will need to be prepared to meet the rising demand for process services on the counselor's level to address the increasing complexity of information use.

When an existing reference service or instructional program incorporates a process dimension into the established service, there must be a clear delineation of a new direction and not just an alternative way of articulating the traditional approach. That new direction requires that emphasis be placed on the process of information use and strategies designed for intervention in the earliest stages of exploration and formulation. An ongoing dialogue would engage the counselor in the user's unfolding information problem or topic.

It is in the early uncertain stages of the search process that the counselor's services are particularly essential. The counselor guides users in acknowledging, expecting, and tolerating feelings of uncertainty and anxiety by assuming an invitational mood. The counselor enables the user to understand the tasks of exploring and formulating as integral to the early stages of information seeking.

The counselor level of intervention addresses the full range of experience in the constructive process of seeking meaning within the information environment. The counselor is an essential role for librarians and information professionals in the information age.

## STRATEGIES FOR IMPLEMENTING A PROCESS APPROACH

The counselor's role is becoming a critical component of services in all types of libraries. There are some practical strategies for implementing a process approach to information counseling services. Process strategies can be adapted for a wide range of library users, from the youngest child in a school library to the most sophisticated patron of a research library.

The most important first step in counseling users is to become keenly aware of different stages in the process of learning from information access and use. Begin listening for clues of early stages of uncertainty in a person's vague descriptions of his or her problem or topic. Become aware of the undertones and the mood of comments and questions. Be alert to signs of confusion, frustration, and doubt. This undertone of uncertainty is not limited to work and education related information needs, but may be apparent in more leisure-oriented pursuits as well. The constructive process of seeking meaning pervades every aspect of human endeavor. Ignorance of the process of seeking meaning frequently underlies the limited choices that people make.

Three main strategies for counseling are charting, composing, and conversing. Charting enables the user to visualize the total search process from initiation to closure and to anticipate what to expect in each stage of the process. Composing and conversation go hand in hand to enable the user to focus or formulate a point of view. They comprise a means of documenting and organizing for presentation and application. Conversing enables the user to articulate thoughts, identify gaps, and clarify inconsistencies in the process of the search.

**Charting**

The timeline of the Information Search Process developed in the research described in this book (see Table 3–2) may be adopted as an instrument for illustrating the process to library users. The diagram enables users to visualize a sequence of stages in information seeking. The counselor may use this chart as a basis for determining the stage that the user is experiencing and to describe the overall process to the user. The timeline can be simply drawn on a piece of paper or prepared as a formal handout. The objective is for users to understand the process and to analyze and decide at what stage they would place themselves in the sequence.

Conceptual mapping techniques may be applied to charting information and to visualizing emerging ideas. Conceptual maps organize ideas and show connections between disparate concepts in a similar way that outlining does, but with more visual elements. A simple conceptual map would begin with a circle or box containing the general topic or main idea. Surrounding circles or boxes would be added as related concepts, with lines and arrows connecting the elements in a meaningful display. The visual, nonlinear aspect of conceptual mapping fosters the creative process of connecting ideas and organizing information as a search progresses.

The timeline and flowchart techniques described in Chapter 6 may be adapted for counseling users in charting their own searches. These instruments are most effective for reviewing a recently completed search with a user and reflecting on what went well and what might be improved. However, they may be adapted as planning instruments as well. The timeline and flowchart reveal different aspects of the search process. The timeline is useful for eliciting thoughts that evolve on a topic in the search process. The flowchart is useful for revealing a sequence of sources encountered and used in the progression of a search. Together, they offer two views of this complex, integrated process and enable users to understand their own experience in information seeking.

Surveys conducted at intervals, also, provide a way for users to chart their own search and to track changes in their understanding of both their topic and their search process. The Process Surveys described in Chapter 6 may be used to record users' responses at three points in the search process: initiation, midpoint, and closure. Users may compare the responses that they made at the various points to gain a sense of changes in their thoughts, actions, and feelings as the search progressed.

## Composing

Composing promotes thinking and journal writing is an excellent technique for advancing formulation in the search process. Counselors may recommend that users keep a research journal in which they record ideas, questions, and connections as they progress through their search. Writing in a research journal is much more comprehensive than joting notes on notecards or in a notebook. The journal is started when the project is first initiated, but the purpose changes as the search progresses. Users are instructed to set aside 10 or 15 minutes each day or every few days to write about their problem or topic. Instructions might be stated in the following manner;

> In early stages when you are deciding on what topic to choose, write to clarify or define possible choices. Write about conversations you have about your topic. As you proceed in the process write your reactions to your readings as well as your thoughts and questions about your topic. Be sure to record all incidents where you made an important decision or discovery. Include the development of a central theme, a point of view or focus in your thinking. Record any deadend

of a path or change in the problem or topic which prompted a new approach.

Users may find it helpful to share their journals with the counselor or they may want to keep their writings exclusively for their own reflective use. The main objective of the journal is to serve as a tool for formulating thoughts and developing constructs.

Counselors may also recommend free writing as a means of assisting formulation. Users are encouraged to write about the focus of their topic or problem at several different points in the search process. These pieces of writing promote private reflection which can help users to make connection and inferences in the information they encountered and to see gaps which need further investigation. When these writings are shared with the counselor they can form a basis for deeper understanding of the user's evolving information need.

## Conversing

Conversations and interviews encourage users to discuss the search process from their own particular perspective. Counselors may encourage dialogue by drawing from the user's dynamic process through invitational, exploratory questioning: What ideas seem particularly important to you? What particular questions do you have and what problems are emerging? What is the focus of your thinking and what are the guiding ideas for your search? What are the gaps in your thinking and what inconsistencies do you notice in the information you have encountered?

Charting and composing strategies are an excellent basis for conversing with users. The timeline of the Information Search Process is particularly useful for initiating a conversation about the process that the user is experiencing or is likely to experience. The counselor can discuss the sequence of stages in the process with the user and come to some agreement on what stage the user is in. Conversation provides an opportunity for the counselor to acknowledge feelings commonly associated with the particular stage that the user is experiencing. For example, if a selection or exploration stage is identified the counselor would say something like "you are probably feeling somewhat uncertain and a bit anxious at this point, most people do." If a collection stage is identified the counselor's comments would be directed toward the user's personal perspective and particular area of interest.

A counselor should use caution in discussing the stages of the search process, and be careful not to belabor the issue beyond the point of being helpful to the user. Merely acknowledging the presence of confusion and uncertainty at the beginning and recommending strategies for proceeding is usually sufficient to get a person started. It is important, however, to suggest that some ongoing assistance may be helpful and to offer an invitation to schedule sessions or meetings for counseling throughout the process.

Conversation gives the counselor an opportunity to listen to the user and to recommend appropriate strategies for working through the particular stage in the process that the user is experiencing. Diagnosis of the user's stage is important since formulation of a focused perspective is the turning point in the search. The counselor recommends different strategies before and after the formulation of a focus. Prior to formulation a more invitational approach to searching is recommended; there might be exploratory reading and reflecting in order to better understand the problem. Following formulation a more focused approach of documenting and organizing in order to solve the problem is recommended.

In the early stages, counselors guide users away from overly indicative strategies that narrow the inquiry without exploring the broader prospects. After a focused perspective has been formed, counselors guard against overly invitational strategies that continue gathering general information rather than limiting the search to information pertinent to the focused perspective. Counseling in the stages of the search process guide users through the entire sequence of starting, exploring, focusing, gathering, and closing.

## Recalling, Summarizing, Paraphrasing, and Extending

Counselors encourage people to chart, compose, and converse in order to formulate the ideas that they find important in the information they have encountered. In addition, users may be counseled to use four basic abilities: recalling, summarizing, paraphrasing, and extending.

Recalling is thinking and remembering certain features of what has been gathered and read. Memory plays a critical function in the process of using information. With our limited capacity for recall, we remember selectively rather than recalling everything. Recall is based on our former constructs (world view) which form a frame of reference for selective remembering. What is recalled is a selective process that may differ from person to person. Eliciting personal histories and narratives which relate to the problem are essential for counseling users in selecting that which has some personal meaning. Counselors may guide users to make connections with what they already know and to note what fits or contradicts their view.

Summarizing is organizing ideas in capsulized form and placing the ideas in a meaningful sequence. Summarizing orders ideas and events pulling out salient points or main themes. Not telling all—only what is important—requires an ability to decide what is relevant or pertinent from an individual point of view. Like recalling, summarizing involves selective attention and is based on the person's former constructs. What will be left out is as important a decision as what will be retained. For insight into the complexity of this ability, note how small children want to tell all and have great difficulty choosing parts of a story or event. The decision of what is enough to convey meaning is the difficult conceptual task of formulation. Summarizing involves mentally organizing the information encountered. Our constructs lead us to consider certain ideas as significant and others as less so. There is no one right way to summarize texts. As revealed in the transactional theory of reading, a reader's summary of a text may not match that of an author's. In addition, one reader is likely to summarize quite differently from another. The main objective of summarizing is to organize the information in an abbreviated form by determining ideas that convey meaning. Summarizing prepares information for use by enabling the person to formulate ideas from the information. The task of summarizing is to choose, not everything but enough to convey meaning, and not anything but only that which is important, pertinent, significant, and salient to the individual's formulation.

Paraphrasing is retelling in one's own words the information encountered in the search process. The use of language fosters formulation and prepares information for application. Paraphrasing may be used in enabling recall. Conversing or writing about information gathered may jog memory. One point cues another as the telling occurs. In a similar way paraphrasing may also enable summarizing. The story unfolds within the act of telling. The concept behind paraphrasing is that the reader's words are as acceptable as the author's and more appropriate under certain circumstances. The person is encouraged to break away from the text and to tell the story in his or her own way. When paraphrasing is not valued, copying and plagerism frequently result. From the earliest age, children's retelling or paraphrasing need to be valued and encouraged. Assignments should arise from a problem to be solved that requires paraphrasing ideas rather than a contrived directive that prompts copying word for word from a text. In a similar way, counselors for all types of users should encourage paraphrasing information as a means of understanding and guide users to value their own telling as well as that of others. Paraphrasing, however, may lead to assuming an author's ideas as one's own. It is essential that the origin of the idea be credited and documented. Counselors guide users in determinations of when to quote and how to document sources and in the use of paraphrasing as a powerful ability for formulating within the search process.

Extending is taking ideas from information as our own by fitting them in with what is already known. Extending also involves making connections between the ideas within the information and with information from other sources encountered. In this way, thinking about a topic or problem is extended. Extending also encompasses interpreting information and applying it to the problem in the creative process of using information. Extending occurs throughout the search process not merely toward the end of that process. In fact, all four abilities should be thought of as interwoven in all of the stages in the active process of understanding rather than as occurring in a sequence. Extending leads from one stage of the process to the next. As new questions arise further information is needed. In this recursive process the connections lead to formulation of a focused perspective. The counselor develops strategies and techniques for enabling the user to apply recalling, summarizing, paraphrasing, and extending for working through the stages in the Information Search Process.

## THE LIBRARY PROFESSIONAL IN THE INFORMATION AGE

Librarians are in the midst of redefining their mission in the technological age. The long tradition, in all types of libraries, of providing resources for learning, research, enrichment, and enjoyment is being reassessed to respond to changing societal needs. For that rich tradition of library services to be carried into the 21st century, new roles need to be identified and developed.

The mission of the 1980s was to automate and to network library and information services. Access has been dramatically expanded by automation, networking collections, and databases. Operations for providing information and resources have been streamlined by technological applications. While automating and networking continue to be a priority, the mission of the 1990s, and beyond, calls for services that promote the understanding of ever-increasing amounts of information. A mission of library and information services of the 1990s is to counsel people in the use of resources and information for learning, working, and living. It is no longer sufficient for library and information services merely to provide resources and to offer assistance in the location of materials and information. In the technological age, people require services that counsel them in understanding information and guide them in the process of seeking meaning.

The technological age has brought about two major societal changes that profoundly affect library and information services. First, technology professionalizes the workplace. As most middle-level tasks that occupied countless workers have been automated and may be overseen by a few technicians, professional tasks that require decision making and problem solving are increasing. Professionalization, which affects all aspects of work, has considerable impact on library and information services. Many of the tasks associated with information provision, which traditionally have been within the domain of the librarian, have been automated and are now accomplished by the computer.

At the same time, technology has brought about another societal change that challenges the very mission of library and information services. Technology produces vast amounts of information in a rapidly changing environment. An overwhelming amount of information coupled with rapid change produces unpredictability in all aspects of life. Therefore, uncertainty is pervasive in the seemingly certain technological environment. The confrontation between the uncertain person and the certain system requires professional intervention. There is a critical need for professional counseling in seeking meaning and understanding in information.

The library profession has come of age. In the technological age, librarians and information specialists are called to move into a level of professional services that serves people in much the same way as the legal and medical professions. There is need for challenging new roles that go beyond providing information and that facilitate understanding, problem solving, and decision making. Library and information services must meet the challenge of the information rich environment and progress to intervention for mediating, educating, and counseling people as they seek meaning.

# References

American Library Association. (1980). "Policy Statement: Instruction in the Use of Libraries." *Council Document. No. 45.*

Bannister, D., Ed. (1977). *New Perspectives in Personal Construct Theory.* London: Academic Press.

Bartlett, F. C. (1932). *Remembering: a Study of Experimental and Social Psychology.* Cambridge, England: Cambridge University Press.

Bates, M. (1979). "Idea Tactics," *Journal of the American Society for Information Science, 30,* September, 280–289.

Bates, M. (1986). "Subject Access to Online Catalogs: A Design Model," *Journal of the American Society for Information Science, 37,* 357–376.

Belkin, N. J. (1980). "Anomalous State of Knowledge for Information Retrieval," *Canadian Journal of Information Science, 5,* 133–143.

Belkin, N. J. (1984). "Cognitive Models and Information Transfer," *Social Science Information Studies, 4,* 111–130.

Belkin, N. J., and A. Vickery (1985). *"Interaction in Information Systems."* Library and Information Systems Research Report 35. London: British Library.

Belkin, N. J., H. M. Brooks, and R. N. Oddy (1982). "ASK for information retrieval," *Journal of Documentation, 38,* 61–71.

Biggs, J. B. (1976). "Dimensions of Study Behavior," *British Journal of Educational Psychology, 46,* 68–80.

Blackie, E., and J. Smith (1981). "Student Information Needs and Library User Education," *Education Libraries Bulletin, 24,* 16–23.

Borgman, C. (1984). "Psychological research in human-computer interaction," In *Annual Review of Information Science and Technology, 19,* 33–64.

Bruner, J. (1986). *Actual Minds, Possible Worlds.* Cambridge, MA: Harvard University Press.

Bruner, J. (1973). *Beyond the Information Given: Studies in the Psychology of Knowing.* Edited by J. M. Arglin. New York: W. W. Norton & Co.

Bruner, J. (1975). *Toward a Theory of Instruction.* Cambridge MA: Harvard University Press.

Bruner, J. (1977). *The Process of Education.* Cambridge MA: Harvard University Press.

Buckland, M. (1983). *Library Services in Theory and Context.* New York: Pergamon Press.

Dale, E. (1969). *Audiovisual Methods in Teaching.* 3rd. ed. New York: Holt, Rinehart and Winston.

Debons, A. (1975). "An Educational Program for the Information Counselor," In *Proceedings of the 38th American Society for Information Science Annual Meeting, 12,* 63–64.

DeMey, M. (1977). "The Relevance of the Cognitive Paradigm for Information Science," In *Proceedings of the International Research Forum in Information Science,* Copenhagen.

Dervin, B. (1982). "Useful Theory for Librarianship: Communication, Not Information," *Drexel Library Quarterly, 13,* 16–32.

Dervin, B. (1983). *An Overview of Sense-Making Research; Concepts, Methods, and Results to Date.* Seattle, WA: School of Communication, University of Washington.

Dervin, B., and P. Dewdney (1986). "Neutral Questioning: A New Approach to the Reference Interview," *Reference Quarterly, 25,* 506–513.

Dervin, B. and M. Nilan (1986). "Information Needs and Uses," *Annual Review of Information Science and Technology, 21,* 3–33.

Dervin, B., T. L. Jacobsen, and M. S. Nilan (1982). "Measuring Aspects of Information Seeking: A Test of Quantitative/Qualitative Methodology," In *Communication Yearbook, 6,* 419–422.

Dewey, J. (1934). *Art as Experience.* New York: G. P. Putnam's & Sons.

Dewey, J. (1933). *How We Think.* Lexington, MA: Heath & Company.

Dewey, J. (1944). *Democracy and Education.* New York MacMillan Publishing Co.

Dosa, M. L. (1978). "Information Counseling and Policies," *Reference Librarian, 17,* 7–21.

Durrance, J. (1989). Information Needs: Old Song, New Tune," In *Rethinking the Library in the Information Age. Volume II,* edited by A. Mathews Washington, DC: U.S. Department of Education.

Eisenberg, M. B., and R. E. Berkowitz (1990). *Information Problem Solving: Big Six Skills Approach to Library and Information Skills Instruction,* Norwood, NJ: Ablex Publishing Corp.

Elkind, D. (1976). *Child Development and Education: A Piagetian Perspective.* London: Oxford University Press.

Ellis, D. (1989). "A Behavioral Approach to Information Retrieval System Design," *Journal of Documentation, 45,* 171–212.

Emig, J. (1971). *The Composing Process of Twelfth Graders.* Urbana, IL: National Council of Teachers of English, NCTE Research Report No. 13.

Entwistle, N. J. (1981). *Styles of Learning and Teaching.* New York: Wiley and Sons.

Frannson, A. (1984). "Cramming or Understanding? Effects of Intrinsic and Extrinsic Motivation on Approach to Learning and Test Performance," In *Reading in a foreign language*. White Plains, NY: Longman, 86–121.

Ford, N. (1986). "Psychological Determinants of Information Needs: A Small Scale Study of Higher Education Students," *Journal of Librarianship, 18*, 47–62.

George, M. (1990). "Instructional Services," In *American Libraries: Research Perspectives,* edited by M. J. Lynch Chicago, IL: American Library Association.

Glaser, B. C. and A. L. Strauss (1967). *The Discovery of Grounded Theory: Strategies for Qualitative Research.* New York: Aldine Publishing.

Goodman, N. (1984). *Of Mind and Other Matters.* Cambridge, MA: Harvard University Press.

Hall, H. J. (1981). "Patterns in the Use of Information: The Right to Be Different," *Journal of the American Society for Information Science, 32*, 103–112.

Hollnagel, E. and D. D. Woods (1983). "Cognitive Systems Engineering: New Wine in Old Bottles," *International Journal of Man Machine Studies, 18*, 583–600.

Ingwersen, P. (1982). "Search Procedures in the Library Analyzed from the Cognitive Point of View," *Journal of Documentation, 38*, 165–191.

Inhelder, B. and J. Piaget (1958). *The Growth in Logical Thinking: From Childhood to Adolescence.* New York: Basic Books.

Irving, A. (1985). *Study and Information Skills Across the Curriculum.* London: Heinemann Educational Books.

James, R. (1983). "Libraries in the Mind: How Can We See Users' Perceptions of Libraries," *Journal of Librarianship, 15*, 19–28.

James, W. (1890). *The Principles of Psychology.* New York: Henry Holt.

Katz, W. (1987). *Reference Services and Reference Processes. Volume 2 of Introduction to Reference Work.* 5th. ed. New York: McGraw-Hill.

Kelly, G. A. (1963). *A Theory of Personality: The Psychology of Personal Constructs.* New York: W. W. Norton & Co.

Kerlinger, F. N. (1973). *Foundations in Behavioral Research.* New York: Holt, Rinehart & Winston.

Knapp, P. (1966). *The Monteith College Library Experiment.* Metuchen, NJ: Scarecrow Press.

Krikelas, J. (1983). "Information-Seeking Behavior: Patterns and Concepts," *Drexel Library Quarterly, 19*, 5–20.

Kuhlthau, C. C. (1987). "An Emerging Theory of Library Instruction," *School Library Media Quarterly, 16*, 23–28.

Kuhlthau, C. C. (1988a). "Developing a Model of the Library Search Process: Investigation of Cognitive and Affective Aspects," *Reference Quarterly, 28*, 232–242.

Kuhlthau, C. C. (1988b). "Perceptions of the Information Process in Libraries: A Study of Changes from High School through College," *Information Processing and Management, 24*, 419–427.

Kuhlthau, C. C. (1988c). "Longitudinal Case Studies of the Information Search Process of Users in Libraries," *Library and Information Science, 10*, 251–304.

Kuhlthau, C. C. (1989). "The Information Search Process of High-Middle-Low Achieving High School Seniors," *School Library Media Quarterly, 17*, 224–228.

Kuhlthau, C. C. (1991). "Inside the Search Process: Information Seeking from the User's Perspective," *Journal of the American Society for Information Science, 42,* 361–371.

Kuhlthau, C. C. (1985a). "A Process Approach to Library Skills Instruction," *School Library Media Quarterly, 13,* 23–28.

Kuhlthau, C. C. (1985b). *Teaching the Library Research Process.* West Nyack, NY: Center for Applied Research in Education.

Kuhlthau, C. C. (1983). *The Research Process: Case Studies and Interventions with High School Seniors in Advanced Placement English Classes Using Kelly's Theory of Constructs.* Ed. D Dissertation, Rutgers University.

Kuhlthau, C. C. (1981). *School Librarian's Grade by Grade Activities Program.* West Nyack, NY: Center for Applied Research in Education.

Kuhlthau, C. C., R. J. Belvin, and M. W. George (1989). "Flowcharting the Information Search Process: A Method for Eliciting User's Mental Maps." In *Proceedings of the American Society for Information Science 52nd Annual Meeting, 26,* 162–165.

Kuhlthau, C. C., B. J. Turock, M. W. George and R. J. Belvin (1990). "Validating a Model of the Search Process: A Comparison of Academic, Public and School Library Users," *Library and Information Science Research, 12,* 5–32.

Kuhn, T. (1970). *The Structure of Scientific Revolutions.* Chicago, IL: University of Chicago.

Loertscher, D. (1982). "The Second Revolution: A Taxonomy for the 1980's," *Wilson Library Bulletin, 56,* 417–421.

Lindgren, J. (1981). "Toward Library Literacy," *Reference Quarterly,* Spring, 233–235.

Lynch, M. J. (1977). "Reference Interviews in Public Libraries," Ph.D. Dissertation, Rutgers University.

Maher, B., ed. (1969). *Clinical Psychology and Personality: The Selected Papers of George Kelly.* New York: John Wiley & Sons.

MacMullin, S. E. and R. S. Taylor (1984). "Problem Dimensions Information Traits," *The Information Society, 3,* 91–111.

Mancall, J., S. Aaron, and S. Walker (1986). "Educating Students to Think: The Role of the School Library Media Program," *School Library Media Quarterly, 15,* 18–27.

Marton, F. and F. Saljo (1976). "On Qualitative Differences in Learning," *British Journal of Educational Psychology, 46,* 4–11.

Meadow, C. T. (1983). "User Adaptation in Interactive Information Retrieval," *Journal of the American Society for Information Science, 34,* 280–291.

Mellon, C. (1986). "Library Anxiety: A Grounded Theory and Its Development," *College & Research Libraries, 47,* 160–165.

Miller, G. A. (1956). "The Magical Number Seven, Plus or Minus Two: Some Limits on Our Capacity for Processing Information," *Psychological Review, 63,* 81–97.

Mokros, H. (1990). Personal Correspondence and Conversation. New Brunswick, NJ, School of Communication, Information and Library Studies, Rutgers University.

Neilson, B. (1982). "Teacher or Intermediary: Alternative Models in the Information Age," *College & Research Libraries, 43,* 183–191.

Pask, G. (1976). "Styles and Strategies of Learning," *British Journal of Educational Psychology, 46,* 128–148.

Prentice, A. (1980). "Information Seeking Patterns of Professionals," *Public Library Quarterly, 2,* 27–60.

Ruben, B. D. (1990). "The Health Caregiver-Patient Relationship: Pathology, Etiology, Treatment. In *Communication and Health,* Edited by E. Ray and L. Donohue Hillsdale, NJ: Lawrence Erlbaum, pp. 51–68.

Saracevic, T., H. Mokros and L. Su (1990). "Nature of Interaction Between Users and Intermediaries in Online Searching: A Qualitative Analysis," *Proceedings of the 53rd ASIS Annual Meeting, 27,* 47–54.

Saracevic, T. (1975). "Relevance: A Review of a Framework for Thinking on the Notion of Information Science," *Journal of the American Society for Information Science, 26,* 178–194.

Schön, D. A. (1982). *The Reflective Practioner: How Professionals Think in Action.* New York: Basic Books.

Shannon, C. E. and W. Weaver (1949). *The Mathematical Theory of Communication.* Urbana, IL: University of Illinois Press.

Shera, J. H. (1972). *The Foundations of Education for Librarianship.* New York: John Wiley & Sons.

Stotsky, S. (1990). "On Planning and Writing Plans — or Beware of Borrowed Theories," *College Composition and Communication, 41,* 37–57.

Stripling, B. and J. Pitts (1988). *Brainstorms and Blueprints: Teaching Library Research as a Thinking Process.* Englewood, CO: Libraries Unlimited.

Taylor, R. S. (1991). "Information Use Environments," In *Progress in Communication Sciences* Norwood, NJ: Ablex Publishing Corp., pp. 217–255.

Taylor, R. S. (1962). "The Process of Asking Questions," *American Documentation, 13,* 391–396.

Taylor, R. S. (1968). "Question-Negotiation and Information Seeking in Libraries," *College & Research Libraries, 29,* 178–194.

Taylor, R. S. (1986). *Value Added Processes in Information Systems.* Norwood, NJ: Ablex Publishing Corp.

Tuckett, H. W., and C. J. Stoffle (1984). "Learning Theory and the Self-Reliant Library Users," *Reference Quarterly, 24,* 58–66.

Vickery, B. C., and A. Vickery (1981). *Information Science in Theory and Practice.* London: Butterworths.

Vygotsky, L. (1978). *Mind in Society: The Development of Higher Psychological Processes.* Cambridge, MA: Harvard University Press.

Warriner, J. E. and F. Griffith (1973). *English Grammar and Composition.* New York: Harcourt Brace Jovanovich.

Whittemore, B. and M. C. Yovits (1973). "A Generalized Conceptual Development for the Analysis and Flow of Information," *Journal of the American Society for Information Science, 24,* May-June, pp. 221–231.

Wilson, P. (1977). *Public Knowledge, Private Ignorance: Toward a Library and Information Policy.* Westport, CT: Greenwood Press.

Wilson, T. D. (1981). "On User Studies and Information Needs," *Journal of Documentation, 367,* 3–15.

Yerkes, R. and J. D. Dodson (1908). "The Relation of Strength of Stimulus to Rapidity of Habit Formation," *Journal of Comparative and Neurological Psychology, 18,* 459–482.

Yovits, M. C. and C. R. Foulk (1985). "Experiments and Analysis of Information Use and Value in a Decision Making Context," *Journal of the American Society for Information Science, 36,* 63–81.

Zuboff, S. (1988). *The Age of the Smart Machine.* New York: Basic Books.

# Author Index

# Subject Index

197

Questionnaires, xxiii, 34, 65, 87–90, 100–101, 103–4

**R**

Redundancy, 26–30, 49, 116–18
Redundancy Corollary, 116–18, 125, 173
Reference interview, 9–10
Reference questions, 9, 139–43
Reference service, xix, 9–11
Reference sources, 11, 56, 70
Reflective thinking, 17–19, 30–31, 111
Relevance, 3–4, 8, 39, 49, 121
Research assignments, 33–37, 40, 42, 55, 66–75, 82, 150, 153, 164–65
Research process, *see* Information Search Process
Roles, *see* Advisor (role); Counselor (role); Identifier (role); Instructor (role); Lecturer (role); Locator (role); Organizer (role); Tutor (role)

**S**

Schema Theory, 24
School library media centers, xxiv, 11–12, 33–53, 54–63, 93–102, 152
Search closure, 37, 49, 165
Search logs, 83–84
Search process, *see* Information Search Process
Strategies, *see* Intervention strategies; Process strategies
Selection (stage), xxiii, 35, 73, 118, 122, 136, 170
Sense-making, 3–4, 8, 20, 24, 69, 76

Skill, transference of, 91, 167
Sources, *see* Information sources
Students, 145–54
college, 58–63
high school, xx, xxii, xxiv, 33–53, 54–63, 82, 93–104
Surveys, 58–60, 94, 96–99

**T**

Task, xxiii, xxiv, 22, 38–39, 52, 61–63, 72, 92, 114, 119–20
Taylor, Robert S., 6, 31–32
Teaching role, 145–54, 167; *see also* Counselor (role); Instructor (role); Lecturer (role); Tutor (role)
Theory-building, xix–xx, 3–9, 14–32, 108–27
Thoughts, xxii, 6, 8, 17, 26, 28, 38, 41, 55, 58–63, 91–92
Timelines, 86–87, 91, 105–6
Topic, *see* Information problem
Tutor (role), xxv, 150, 160, 175

**U**

Uncertainty principle, xxv, 8–9, 108–27, 164, 172
Understanding, *see* Sense-making
Uniqueness, 26–30, 116–18
User education, *see* Instruction

**Z**

Zone of intervention, xxvi, 155–62, 175–77
Zone of treatment, 156–60